# Wicked Charleston

# Wicked Charleston

## The Dark Side of the Holy City

Mark R. Jones

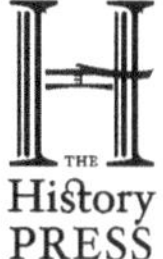
The History Press

Published by The History Press
Charleston, SC 29403
www.historypress.net



*All cover images courtesy of the Library of Congress:*
*King Street, looking north, Charleston, S.C.*
*Lady of the night*, circa 1928
*Symptoms of a duel*, 1839
*New York City Deputy Police Commissioner John A. Leach, right, watching agents pour liquor into sewer following a raid during the height of prohibition*, 1921?
*Social qualities of our candidate*
*The teamsters' duel/sketched by Alfred R. Waud*, 1863

First published 2005
Second printing 2006
Third printing 2008
Fourth printing 2008
Fifth printing 2010
Sixth printing 2012

978-1-59629-076-1
Library of Congress Cataloging-in-Publication Data

Jones, Mark R. (Mark Rowell), 1959-
Wicked Charleston : the dark side of the holy city / Mark R. Jones.
p. cm.
Includes bibliographical references (p. ).
ISBN 1-59629-076-5 (alk. paper)
1. Charleston (S.C.)--Moral conditions--History--17th century. 2. Charleston (S.C.)--Moral conditions--History--18th century. 3. Charleston (S.C.)--Moral conditions--History--19th century. I. Title.
HN80.C43J66 2005
975.7'915--dc22
2005024246

# Contents

# Contents

# Acknowledgements

I must thank John LaVerne of Bulldog Tours for giving me the opportunity to give tours for the number one walking-tour company in Charleston. John is a unique boss. He hires tour guides and allows them the freedom to give *their* tour, and not a scripted, corporate-approved lecture. It is a freedom that I cherish and take seriously.

Secondly, I must thank John for allowing me to take all my research for The Dark Side of Charleston walking tour and turn it into this book. He has been completely supportive during the entire process of researching and writing this book. Thanks a thousand times over, John.

There are at least six other tour guides who give the Dark Side tour for Bulldog. This book is in no way intended to be reflective of their tours. This book is my version of Charleston's darker side. Each of the other guides has their own particular focus for their tour, each entertaining and informative. Again, that is the atmosphere that John LaVerne creates in his company. All of us are free to make the tour what we wish.

I also must thank Tom, Tommy and Ben Doyle of Palmetto Carriage Works. The Doyles hired me in 2001 as a carriage driver/tour guide and introduced me to what has become my professional life. Without their initial support and training I may have never discovered my perfect career. Thanks to the Doyles for giving me the freedom to juggle my commitment to their company with my interest in the dark side of Charleston. One of my favorite facts I discovered during my research is that on the present location of Palmetto Carriage's big red barn, Cornell June ran a brothel that kept "between six and fifteen women in service against their will."

A big thanks also goes to my friend and co-worker at Palmetto Carriage and Bulldog Walking Tours, Jim Brain. We became tour guides at the same time and Jim has always been my best sounding board for ideas and information. Day after day, Jim proves that his last name is no fluke.

A special thanks to the old codger himself—J. Francis Brenner. The two hours I spent listening to Mr. Brenner reminisce about Charleston of the early twentieth century was spellbinding. Here's to his continued health.

And finally, biggest thanks of all must go to my wife Teresa. She is the first to hear my ideas and shoot them down, which most of them deserve. She was the first reader (and editor) of this manuscript and has a developed a hatred of my misplaced commas and semicolons. Without her support, patience, love and guidance, this book may have never been finished. It would have been a lesser effort without her input—as everything else in my life would be. Thanks sweetie! I owe you a meal at the Charleston restaurant of your choosing.

# Part One

# Eat, Drink and Be Merry—Early Charleston

# Chapter One
# The Merry Monarch

*A man with an erection heeds no advice.*
Samuel Pepys, member of the Royal Court—1662.

## King Charles II—The Merry Monarch

During the settling of the American colonies, it was said that the Spaniards would first build a church, the Dutch would first build a fort and the English a tavern. Welcome to Charleston, an English colony founded in 1670.

It was first called Charles Town, named after King Charles II. Charles Town was founded after the end of the English Revolution, also called the Puritan Revolution, the general designation for the period in English history from 1640 to 1660. The English Revolution proceeded through two civil wars, the trial and execution of King Charles I, the republican experiments of Oliver Cromwell and, ultimately, the restoration of King Charles II.

The revolution was provoked by the behavior of Charles I. Charles believed in the divine right of kings and did not hold himself accountable to Parliament. The immediate cause of the conflict, however, was

Charles's attempt to impose the Anglican liturgy in Scotland in 1637. The Presbyterian Scots rioted and raised an army to defend their church. In 1640, their army occupied the northern counties of England.

Charles summoned the Long Parliament to raise money in support of his war against the Scots. They met in November 1640 and demanded reforms from Charles as the price for their support. The political quarrel soon became an armed conflict with most of the Lords and a few members of the House of Commons siding with the king.

Oliver Cromwell, a Puritan and a member of Parliament, led his forces to victory against the army of King Charles I. Even though he had no prior military experience, Cromwell was a brilliant leader and by the end of 1648 the king was defeated. Charles was convicted of treason by Parliament and beheaded on January 30, 1649. This left Cromwell as virtual dictator of England. Being a Puritan, Cromwell instituted the typical Puritanical doctrine: no fun allowed—no drinking, no gambling, no dancing and, absolutely, positively no wenching. Under the rule of Cromwell, it was not jolly old England.

Meanwhile, Charles's son, Charles II, assumed the title of king and was so proclaimed in Scotland, sections of Ireland and in England, even though Cromwell ruled the country. Charles spent eight years, most of them in Paris, in exile on the continent.

While a young man in Paris, Charles had a vigorous sexual appetite. He spent many hours in establishments called *maisons des baigneurs*, where a man could go to be "tended and cherished, and could indulge oneself in all pleasure offered by the luxury and depravity of a great city."

In 1658, following the death of Cromwell, the demand for the restoration of royalty increased. On April 23, 1661, Charles was crowned king. In retribution of what had been done to his father, Charles II ordered all the Cromwellians who had condemned his father to be rounded up and executed. Also, on January 30, 1661, twelve years to the day after his father had been beheaded, Charles II had Cromwell's body exhumed from its splendid tomb in Westminster Abbey and publicly hanged. The "twice dead" body was then decapitated, the torso buried beneath the gallows and his head stuck on a pike in front of Westminster Hall.

The reign of Charles II came to be known as the era of "eat, drink and be merry." England became known as jolly old England, and Charles picked up the nickname "The Merry Monarch." Samuel Pepys described the court of King Charles II "as there being so much...swearing, drinking and whoring that I do not know what will be the end of it." Royal promiscuity became legend, including stories about the size of the king's penis. The royal penis was described by one participant of a court orgy as being as the size of His Majesty's scepter. Pepys, a loyal member of the royal court, described Charles's relationship with women as such: "The King doth spend most of his time in feeling and kissing them naked all over their bodies in bed...this lechery will never leave him."

One of Charles's lovers was Countess Barbara Palmer Castlemaine, a woman who would drink, gamble and talk filthy with men. She was also ambitious and domineering. Charles seemed blind with lust for Castlemaine and often performed public sexual acts with her. Pepys summed up their relationship by commenting: "A man with an erection heeds no advice."

Castlemaine was herself a sexual deviant. According to Lord Coleraine, she once dined on the corpse of a deceased bishop and devoured "as much of the priviteeas the lady could get into her mouth." She took great pleasure in despoiling a man of God even after his death.

One of the king's most famous mistresses was Nell Gwynn. Born in the slum of Coal Yard Alley, Gwynn was a natural beauty, and at age thirteen she found work at the King's Theatre and quickly became a favorite. Pepys, an avid theatre-goer, became enchanted with her. It was not just her acting that attracted him. He described Nell as "a bold merry slut" with a bold laugh and quick dirty tongue. Within weeks of meeting her, Charles began to send for her, and soon moved her into a house in the Pall Mall district. It didn't take long for a local poet to come up with this ditty:

*Hard by Pall Mall lives a wench call'd Nell.*
*King Charles the Second he kept her.*
*She hath got a trick to handle his prick.*
*So she never lays hands on his scepter.*

Just within his court and private circle Charles sired twelve bastard children with seven women. He fathered five with Castlemaine, two with Nell and one child each with five other women. The number of bastards he sired out of court with more than fifty women has been estimated as between thirty-five and one hundred.

## Lord Anthony Ashley Cooper—the Greatest Whoremaster

Born July 22, 1621, Anthony Ashley Cooper served in the Short Parliament in 1640 as a supporter of the Puritan Oliver Cromwell. At the start of the English Revolution, Ashley Cooper switched his political support to Charles I and the Royalists. He subsequently became an important member of the so-called Cabal, an elite advisory group serving King Charles II. In 1660, he was made privy councilor and in 1661 was appointed Chancellor of the Exchequer. In 1672, he was named the first Earl of Shaftesbury.

Cooper had an "addiction to the brothels," according to his contemporaries. "His open lewdness he could ne'er disguise," wrote John Dryden. Cooper was known as a man who "loves fumbling with a Wench, with all his heart."

Once he became a public man, his reputation for prostitutes became such public knowledge that by 1679 there were considerable references to Cooper's lewd behavior in plays performed in England. Once, while Cooper was serving as Lord Chancellor for Charles II, he entered the royal hall and was greeted by Charles with the remark: "Here comes the greatest whoremaster in England."

To reward some of his longtime loyal supporters, Charles II gave eight men (called the Lords Proprietors) a land grant to the Carolina colony, which included everything south of Virginia to Florida and everything west to the Pacific Ocean. One hell of a gift! Cooper became the leader of the Proprietors and is the man whom historians credit as the driving force behind the founding of the Carolina colony. Anthony Ashley Cooper's value to Charleston today is honored by the two rivers that border the peninsula, the Ashley and the Cooper.

With the assistance of John Locke, his brilliant young secretary, Cooper was responsible for the Fundamental Constitutions of Carolina, the document outlining Cooper's vision for the colony. Thus, the "greatest whoremaster in England" created one of the most liberal and revolutionary documents of his era.

The Fundamental Constitutions argued for the concept of government for the good of the public and advocated the most liberal religious policy of any American colony. Cooper and Locke decreed that in order to own land every freedman in Carolina must acknowledge the existence of God and the need for public and solemn worship. In order to have the benefit of these laws each colonist over the age of seventeen had to be a member of some religious congregation. However, the document also stated that "any Seven or more Persons agreeing in any Religion, shall constitute a Church." Cooper felt that this liberal policy would allow Indians as well as Europeans of differing persuasions to live together in harmony. No member of any church was to "disturb or molest" any rival religious assembly. The policy of "Seven or more Persons agreeing" was often interpreted to include a gathering in a tavern. What a great idea! It was once legally possible in Charles Town to belly up to the bar and be in church at the same time.

The legal groundwork was ready for the settling of Charles Town. All that was needed were colonists.

## Addicted to Rum

During the first week of April 1670, the first 147 colonists arrived on three ships under the leadership of Captain Joseph West. Some of the provisions on board included four thousand gallons of beer and thirty gallons of brandy. They found, as Walter J. Fraser writes, the "Water about Town so brackish that it is scarcely potable unless mixed with... liquors."

Seven months later, Captain West complained that many of the settlers "were so addicted to the Rum, that they will do little whilst the bottle is at their nose." Ten years later the council felt it necessary to pass an act for "the Suppression of Idle, Drunken and Swearing Persons" and to "prohibit entrance of punch houses, or tippling houses during time of Divine Service." The council finally figured it out—people were going to taverns for worship instead of church. It was the first time, but not the last, that Charles Town politicians would try to pass a law to direct people away from the bars and into the churches.

Many of the colonists were indentured servants, male and female. The indentured servant signed a contract with a landowner, sometimes known as a Master, who paid for their passage to America. For the length of the contract (usually three to five years) the servant worked for the Master. At the end of the contract the servant was free and given fifty acres of land. Many of the female indentured servants discovered a quicker route out of servitude—prostitution. Sleep with your Master, and the length of your contract would be reduced. After these female servants were out of their contracts, many discovered the easiest path to a substantial income was to continue their role as a prostitute. Thus, the establishment of workingwomen in Charleston began early.

Some of those workingwomen plied their trade at an early rum house called the Bowling Green House, in the vicinity of the present-day corner of Anson and Hasell Streets (possibly the current site of St. Johannes Lutheran Church). In the Bowling Green House, sailors and Indians could be found "tyed by the Lipps to a pewter engine" of beer, rum punch, brandy and Madeira wine, consuming as much as "£16 at one Bout." Sailors and wenches were so notorious for causing disorders that the men of the Night Watch (police) were empowered to apprehend and hold until morning any seaman frequenting a public house after dark.

During the first three decades many public officials (members of the council) were removed from office for scandalous behavior, which usually included public drunkenness and "lying [*sic*] with wenches." The clergy offered little help. The first Anglican minister, Reverend Atkin Williamson, was dismissed in 1681 for baptizing a bear while drunk.

By the beginning of the eighteenth century, the population of Charles Town totaled 4,000, with 1,700 Anglicans, 1,300 Presbyterians, 500 French Huguenots, 400 Baptists and 100 Quakers. While almost 50 percent of Charles Town residents were Anglican, the remainder were labeled dissenters, being members of any Protestant religion other than the official Church of England.

Even though every citizen was (officially) a member of a congregation, public officials complained about the immoral atmosphere infecting the city. In May 1703, the assembly considered legislation to prevent "Mens Cohabitating with women with whom they ware not married & against Strumpets" and passed an "Act against Bastardy."

The clergy were swimming against a tide of sin. They agreed the behavior of the citizens was "ungodly," but that was their only common ground. Most dissenters considered the entire Anglican Church scandalous, and many Anglicans agreed. They hoped that their new commissary would strengthen the reputation of the Church in Carolina.

There was never a bishop in the colonies, and all colonials came under the authority of the bishop of London. The bishop would appoint a commissary who would exercise most of the functions of a bishop. The Church Act of 1706 divided the settled sections of the Carolina colony into ten parishes, and the parish church was supposed to serve as the center of local culture.

In 1708, a ship set sail from England bound for Charles Town and carrying the appointed commissary to the colony, Reverend Gideon Johnston. As was customary before making the long passage across the Atlantic during a trip from England to Carolina, the ship stopped to re-supply off the coast of Portugal at the island of Madeira. Johnston went ashore and he sampled a new drink—a golden-colored spirit named after the very island. Madeira wine is aged at least twenty years in casks and then bottled and allowed to mature for another thirty to seventy-five years.

The reverend enjoyed the wine so much that he missed the departure of his ship. He arranged for a second departure and persuaded the captain to load several cases of Madeira to enjoy during the voyage. Johnston's second ship arrived in Charles Town without the reverend on board. He was found marooned on an island off the coast without food and water—apparently abandoned by the ship's crew. Madeira soon became the drink of choice among the Charles Town elite. Currently, there is a brand of Madeira on the market called "Charleston."

Once he arrived in Charles Town, Johnston had to deal with many problems including his predecessor at St. Philip's Church, Reverend Edward Marston, who was angry that he had been replaced. Marston often followed Johnston around town calling him an "Irish bandit." However, Marston was forced to flee town after being arrested for a public fistfight and for fraud and indebtedness.

Johnston also had to deal with ministers of other faiths. The minister of the Scotch-Presbyterian church called St. Philip's "a scandalous church" from his pulpit. The minister of the Baptist congregation, William Screven, was a carpenter by trade. Johnston looked down on Screven, since he was not a trained cleric but just a mere carpenter. Johnston called Screven "extremely ignorant."

# Judge Trott—Two Cases: Witchcraft and Murder

Judge Nicholas Trott, the son of London merchant Samuel Trott, was born in London, England. Trott's paternal grandfather, Perient Trott, was a director of the Somers Island Company, the company formed to colonize Bermuda. His uncle Nicholas Trott, sometimes called "Nicholas the elder," was a governor of the Bahamas, and during his tenure Bermuda became notorious as a safe haven for pirates. The younger Trott is sometimes confused with him, but unlike his uncle, "Nicholas the younger" had no love for pirates, and when the occasion presented itself he dealt with them ruthlessly.

Trott's family connections helped him obtain the posts of secretary to the Somers Island Company and attorney general of Bermuda in 1693. In 1699, Trott arrived in Charles Town to become attorney general and naval officer. Historian M. Eugene Sirmans called Trott "the most learned man in the colony."

Trott's political and legal career in Charles Town was controversial due to his political and religious partisanship. When Trott publicly criticized Governor Joseph Blake, he was arrested and excluded from office. In 1702, at the insistence of the colonial assembly, the governor and council restored him to his former positions, and one year later promoted him to chief justice of the colony. For several years thereafter, Trott was actively involved in the efforts of the dominant Anglican clique to establish the Church of England and to suppress dissenters. Trott was a devout adherent of the Church of England and an early and faithful member of the Society for the Propagation of the Gospel (SPG).

Trott and his brother-in-law William Rhett were influential in the colonial assembly. From 1711 to 1715, Trott and Rhett, who was then speaker of the assembly, expanded their powers over the Charles Town electorate, which elected the majority of the assembly members. In 1714, while on a visit to England, Trott was granted several extraordinary legal powers by the Proprietors: the right to appoint the provost marshal; the necessity of his presence for a quorum in the colonial council; and the final word on proposed laws. In fact, no law could become valid without his approval.

Trott returned to Charles Town as the most powerful man in the colony, with the personal blessing of the Proprietors. By this time, he and Rhett controlled virtually all of the royal and proprietary offices in South Carolina. Their greatest achievement during this period was Rhett's hunt and arrest of the Gentleman Pirate, Stede Bonnet, and his crew, and Trott's subsequent conviction and execution of the pirates.

By 1719, however, due to his influence in all matters, Trott was thoroughly detested by his Charles Town contemporaries. A formal complaint to the Proprietors was lodged against him, charging that he collected exorbitant fees in his courts, multiplied fees by delays in the proceedings, abused his office as judge by advising parties in cases pending before him and monopolized the colony's political and judicial offices.

Opposition to Trott and Rhett, as strong as it was, apparently played no role in the political upheaval that ended proprietary government in 1719. One cause of the revolution was the Proprietors' failure to provide adequately for the danger to the colony posed by the Indians and pirates. The colonists persuaded the Parliament to send both protection and a royal governor, Francis Nicholson. Nicholson reappointed all proprietary officeholders except Trott, who sought in vain to continue as chief justice. From 1719 until his death, Trott devoted himself to private life as a scholar and writer; his most popular work was *The Tryals of Major Stede Bonnet and Other Pirates* (1719).

During his tenure, Justice Trott had the full force of English law behind him and penalties were harsh. For stealing, a person could be sentenced to a public whipping, a burning of the hand, a cropping of an ear or, depending on the value of the theft, death. Horse thieves were usually executed or whipped and maimed. Murder was always dealt with by an "eye for an eye" sentence—execution. The preferred method of execution was hanging, but there are numerous instances of public burnings, particularly when blacks were the accused.

Hangings were social occasions with a carnival atmosphere. Once the "dead warrant" was signed by the court, the provost marshal erected a gallows. On the appointed day of execution, the condemned man's family followed him to the gallows. At this time the condemned addressed the hundreds of citizens gathered, giving a biographical sketch of his life, which usually concluded by declaring his guilt or innocence. Then he was executed. Food and drink were usually sold to the public. When the body dropped, drinks were raised and cheers echoed.

Trott presided over every important case held in Charles Town for almost twenty years. Including the trial of a witch, and the first sensational murder trial.

Reverend Dr. Francis Le Jau, an SPG missionary, in a letter dated April 14, 1707, to Philip Stubbs, secretary of the SPG, wrote: "A notorious Malefactor evidently guilty of Witchcraft & who has kill'd several persons by the Devils help was lately return'd by the Grand Jury." Five months later, in another letter to Stubbs, Le Jau mentions the case again:

> *The last Sedition begun while the Judge was examining Evidence relating to the accused Witch that is still in our Prisons...she said she will come off and that she has many powerful friends here. It is a dismal Sight to perceive how powerfully the Spirit of the Devil is here.*

A woman had been arrested and charged with witchcraft. According to witnesses, several persons "had become ill & 2 dyed" due to the witch's charms. She was imprisoned for fifteen months before she was brought to trial before Justice Trott. Trott's charge to the grand jury in the Witchcraft Trial—1707:

> *Now because this is a matter that will come before* [you]*: and being a thing of great difficulty. I must therefore pray your Patience & diligent Attention, till I speak something largely to it.*
>
> *We live in an Age of Atheism & Infidelity, and some Persons that are no great Friends to Religion, have made it their Business to decry all Stories of Apparitions and of Witches...for if their* [sic] *be such Creatures as Witches then there is certainly Spirits by whose aid & Assistance they Act, and by consequence then there is an other invisible world of Spirits...that there is such creatures as Witches I make no doubt, neither do I think that they can be denyed, without denying the truth of the holy Scriptures. Now that the Scriptures do affirm that there are Witches & Magicians, is evident, from so many Places... that time will not permit me now to recite them to You.*
>
> *I shall therefore only produce two or three Testimonies from them & vindicate the truty* [sic] *of the Translation & the Sense of them... that ye denyers of Witchcraft have endeavored to put upon them.*

Trott then takes twenty manuscript pages to "prove" to the grand jury that witches and spirits exist. To make his case he first quotes Biblical sources:

> Deuteronomy 18: *"There shall not be found among you any one that maketh his Son or Daughter to pass through fire, or that useth divination, or an observer of times, or an enchanter or a Witch. Or a charmer, or a consulter with familiar spirits, or a wizard, or a necromancer. For all that do these things are an abomination to the Lord, and because of these abomoninations, the Lord thy God doth drive them out from before thee.*
>
> *"And the Soul that turneth after such as hath familiar Spirits, & after wizards, to goe a whoring after them.*
>
> *"A man also or woman that hath a familiar Spirit, or that is a wizard, shall surely be put to death; they shall stone them with stones: their blood shall be upon them."*
>
> Exodus 22:18: *"Thou shalt not suffer a witch to live."*

Trott also quotes (translating for the jury) from Hebrew, Greek and Latin texts, citing more than a dozen instances in "ancient and holy writings" that witches and wizards were creatures of flesh and blood.

He continues: "Now...I thinke I have fully proved to you that there are such Creatures as Witches." He then proceeds to explain to the grand jury the English law declaring witchcraft a capital offense against God:

> *Witchcraft in the first degree is defined as an invocation or conjuration of an evil spirit; consulting, having a covenant with, entertaining, employing, feeding or rewarding any evil spirit to any intent; taking up any dead person, or the skin, bone and any part thereof, to be employed or used in witchcraft, charm etc.; or any exercise of any witchcraft, enchantment, charm or sorcery, whereby any person shall be killed or destroyed, consumed or lamed in his or her body.*
>
> *Witchcraft in the second degree is defined as one of the following: taking upon him or them by witchcraft, enchantment, charm or sorcery to tell them where treasure is to be found; or where goods, or things lost, or stolen may be found; or to the intent to provoke any person to unlawful love; whereby good or cattle shall be destroyed; or the use of witchcraft to hurt any person.*

Trott's most sensational trial was when Sarah Dickenson, Edward Beale and Joshua Brenan of Charles Town were brought before the bench and accused of murder.

Mrs. Dickenson and Mr. Beale were both married, but together they were enjoying an adulterous affair. When Beale's wife suddenly died the city was left curious and suspicious. Beale also attempted to ruin his lover's husband by publicly making false accusations against Mr. Dickenson and eventually trying to poison him. The attempt was unsuccessful, so Beale and Mrs. Dickenson hired Joshua Brenan to poison her husband. This time they were successful.

Mrs. Dickenson was charged with murder and accessory before the fact. Beale was charged with five offenses: adultery, false accusations against the deceased, accessory before the fact, accessory after the fact and murder. Brenan was charged with murder. All three were found guilty.

Judge Trott addressed the accused at their sentencing:

> *You the Prisoners at ye Bar, Sarah Dickenson, Edward Beale & Joshua Brenan: You stand here convicted of one of the greatest of Crimes, willful & malitious Murder. A crime which carryes it's own natural Horror and Guilt.*
>
> *As for you Sarah Dickenson you are not only guilty of Murder, but ye Murder of your Husband, him whom you promised at your marriage to Love, cherish & obey: instead of that, not only to conspire his Death, but actually kill him; is a Crime which I cannot think of words bad enough to express it.*
>
> *And for you Edward Beale that have been her Aider, Abetter & Procurer to commit this horrid crime. Consider you murdered the person not because that he had offended you; but because you had offended him. You were not content to rob him of his Wife, and to defile his Bed; (of which your guilt is notoriously known) But such was your malice, that you conspired to take away his Life.*
>
> *In charity to your Soul I cannot omit mentioning to You an other of your Crimes: which is the murder of your own wife. Which I believe in my conscience you have been guilty of. It is true for want of proof, it cannot be fixed upon you: But remember, if you are guilty of it, that you must answer it before God: from whom nothing can be hid.*

> *As for you Joshua Brenan I cannot omit mentioning to You...that, besides the Cruelty & Barbarity with which you murdered the deceased person; that you did it in sight of the Heathen, ye barbarous Indians, and by that means gave them occasion to condemn & blaspheme ye Gospel of Christ.*
>
> *I must now do my Office as a Judge:*
>
> *That you Sarah Dickenson shall goe to the place from whence you came & from thence shall be drawn upon a Hurdle, to the place of Execution, and there shall be burned to Death.*
>
> *And that you Edward Beale & Joshua Brenan shall goe from hence to the place from whence you came, and from thence to the place of Execution, where you will be severely hanged by the Neck, till you are severely dead; And God of infinite mercy be merciful to every one of your Souls.*

These then were the early years of Charles Town: citizens using a loophole in a law to attend divine service in a tavern with six of their friends, one drunk minister who baptized a bear and another who was late arriving to the city due to his love of wine; and of course, witches and adulterers.

Welcome to Charleston—an English colony named after the Merry Monarch who fathered more than one hundred bastard children. The city's two main rivers are named after its most influential founder, who was called "the greatest whoremaster in England" by no greater authority than the Merry Monarch himself. After all, it takes one to know one.

# Chapter Two

# The Sweet Trade and Free Love

*If you had fought like a man, you wouldn't have to be hanged like a dog.*
Female pirate Anne Bonny, to her partner Jack Rackham.

## The Odd Couple: Blackbeard and Stede Bonnet

Pirates were once encouraged in Charles Town. During the first two decades of the eighteenth century pirates preyed on the Spanish galleons carrying gold and other treasure from Florida to Spain. Charles Town tavern owners and shopkeepers embraced those free-spending agents of the sweet trade. However, after 1718 there was an increase of attacks on British ships bound to and from Charles Town, plundering by the likes of Blackbeard, Charles Vane, Calico Jack Rackham and the "Gentleman Pirate" Stede Bonnet.

Bonnet was an unlikely candidate for piracy. He was an educated man and served in the Royal Army as a major. After retirement from the military, he grew wealthy as the owner of a large sugarcane plantation in Barbados. For some reason, in 1717 Bonnet purchased a ship, the *Revenge,* hired a crew of seventy and set sail out of Bridgetown Harbor and began to plunder ships in the Caribbean. This is the *only* recorded incident of a pirate *purchasing* a ship.

No one is sure why Bonnet turned to piracy. One theory is that he suffered from a "disordered mind." Another theory is that he rebelled against his comfortable life and suffered what we would now call a "midlife crisis." Instead of buying a Corvette, he bought a pirate ship. The most enduring and popular theory, however, was that Bonnet turned to the sweet trade to escape his nagging, shrewish wife.

It didn't take Bonnet's crew long to determine that he was not much of a pirate. He suffered from seasickness, dressed in fine clothes and wore a powdered wig. He was a refined gentleman who rarely drank and spent most of his time reading in his cabin. That was not the profile of a typical pirate. The crew was talking mutiny with plans to strand Bonnet on a deserted island when the *Revenge* crossed paths with the infamous Edward Teach—"Blackbeard."

Blackbeard was born in Bristol, England, around 1690. When he was twelve he served as a deckhand aboard a privateer during Queen Anne's War (1702–1713). There was a thin line between being a privateer and a pirate; the only thing that separated the two was a sheet of paper that bore the queen's signature. As a privateer, one had the right to attack enemy ships and, in the name of the queen, seize their cargo called "booty." When there was no war in which they could offer their services, many privateers became pirates.

Blackbeard arrived in Jamaica as a teenager and for the next several years he served his pirate apprenticeship under Captain Benjamin Horningold. Captain Horningold recognized the unique abilities of the young Teach, and began to groom the man as his successor. Piracy was not a long-term career. Most pirates were either arrested or killed, or they retired after a short period of time. The risks were substantial, but profits made during three years of plundering could be enough to set a man up for the rest of his life.

Horningold and Blackbeard captured a two-hundred-ton French slave ship, *Concorde.* It was a substantial windfall. Horningold accepted the king's pardon for his crimes and retired from piracy to a quiet life. As a parting gift he presented his young protégé the slave ship, which Blackbeard renamed *Queen Anne's Revenge.*

Blackbeard was a man of imposing stature. He stood over six feet, two inches and weighed about two hundred and fifty pounds. This was during an era where, due to poor diet in childhood, men rarely grew past five feet, six inches and one hundred pounds. Blackbeard towered above most men. His signature feature was a coarse, thick, wild black mane of facial hair, which he festooned with colorful ribbons. When charging into battle, he weaved lit fuses into his beard so that his face was encircled with a ring of smoke, illuminated by the red glow of hissing fuses. Armed with swords and a trio brace of pistols slung from bandoleers, he looked like a demon from hell—which was his goal. Blackbeard was a master of what we now call "psychological warfare." He knew if he could frighten his opponents they would be less apt to fight a protracted battle.

His normal drink was rum laced with gunpowder. He would light the concoction and drink it down in one gulp, leaving a flame in the glass, his beard singed and smoldering. He delighted in taking two or three crewmen with him into the hold, closing the hatches and lighting several pots of brimstone. He and his crew would sit in the darkness, breathing the stench from the suffocating fumes until one by one the crewmen begged for release. Blackbeard would be the last man to climb from the hold, laughing at their weakness.

Periodically, Blackbeard would kill one of his crew for some minor offense. He claimed that if he "didn't kill one of my men now and then, they would forget who was in charge."

Blackbeard had one weakness though—women. Most pirates used prostitutes while in port, but not Blackbeard. He typically married the girls he wanted. He loved females, but had no intention of committing himself to one woman. While in port, he would pick out a woman in a tavern and bring her on board. He would have another pirate captain perform a wedding ceremony and for the next several weeks, he enjoyed the life of a married man. However, Blackbeard's idea of marriage was quite unusual.

After the "wedding" night it was his custom to force his "wife" to prostitute herself, sometimes at the point of a sword. He would allow the members of his crew, which often numbered over three hundred, to pay for the pleasure of sleeping with the captain's "wife." When he left port, he would leave his "wife" behind. Blackbeard left more than fourteen "wives" scattered throughout Caribbean and south Atlantic coastal cities.

During an eighteen-month period (1717–1718), Blackbeard terrorized the coast from Honduras to Virginia, taking at least twenty prizes, more than one ship per month—an amazing record of plunder. He burned most of the ships he boarded, but added several to his growing fleet.

Most of the American colonies had turned their back on pirates by this time, except North Carolina, which was struggling for economic stability. Blackbeard had an arrangement with the governor of North Carolina, Charles Eden. In exchange for a share of Blackbeard's booty the governor would issue a pardon. Blackbeard and dozens of other pirates found a willing marketplace for their booty in North Carolina.

Blackbeard also discovered a perfect hideout off Ocracoke Island, a place he called Teach's Hole. The Hole was in the midst of the Outer Banks, a bewildering labyrinth of inlets, creeks and islands, which served as a perfect location for pirates to hide from authorities, bury their treasure and refit their ships in complete privacy.

In the early spring of 1718, Stede Bonnet had been conducting business in Charles Town, secretly selling booty to some local merchants who were happy to buy the stolen goods for a fraction of their value. Bonnet was lying off the Charles Town coast planning his next move when Blackbeard's fleet sailed past. Blackbeard came aboard the *Revenge* and met its dandy captain.

An odder couple would be hard to imagine: Blackbeard, brutish and flamboyant with flaming beard and wild hair; and Stede Bonnet, a pudgy little gentleman-dandy wearing snow-white breeches and a powdered wig.

Blackbeard quickly realized that Bonnet's crew was unhappy with their captain. He convinced Bonnet that since the gentleman was inexperienced, and not used to the rigors of pirate command, it would be more productive if they threw in together. Blackbeard offered to put one of his men on board so that Bonnet could live a more relaxed lifestyle on his vessel.

Weeks later, in May 1718, Blackbeard's six-ship pirate fleet blockaded Charles Town harbor, with Bonnet on board the *Revenge* as "captain-of-leisure." The pirates pillaged nine vessels and held several prominent citizens hostage, including Samuel Wragg, a member of the Governor's Council. With these hostages at his mercy, Blackbeard effectively held the city of Charles Town in his control for several days. The pirates freely roamed the city's taverns and brothels, ransacking businesses, sampling merchandise and women, and attacking anyone who put up resistance. As long as the hostages remained in Blackbeard's control the populace was powerless to retaliate. Finally, in exchange for rations, gold and medical supplies, South Carolina Governor Robert Johnson was able to buy the release of the hostages. Blackbeard sailed unmolested out of the harbor with more than £1,500 of gold and silver and made a beeline for Teach's Hole.

Blackbeard advised Bonnet that to make it more difficult for South Carolina authorities to chase them down, it would be better for the pirate fleet to separate. He suggested they lie low for several weeks and explore the possibility of obtaining pardons from the North Carolina governor. Bonnet and ten of his men went ashore to obtain provisions and inquire about the pardons. As soon as they were gone, Blackbeard transferred everything of value onto his vessels, scuttled the *Revenge*, and left the rest of Bonnet's crew stranded on a sand bar. Bonnet returned a week later and discovered what had happened. He rescued his men and set to work repairing the *Revenge*, which he renamed *Royal James*.

After the Blackbeard blockade, Governor Johnson of South Carolina asked Colonel William Rhett to hunt down and capture the pirates terrorizing the Carolina coast. Rhett, a well-proven soldier, outfitted two ships, *Sea Nymph* and *Henry*, with one hundred and thirty men and armament. Governor Johnson then outfitted four more ships and over the next two weeks he personally commanded an expedition to root out other pirates south of Charles Town. Johnson's force killed twenty-six pirates and nineteen others were brought back to town for trial.

With the intention of locating and capturing Blackbeard, Rhett left Charles Town and headed north. Within a week Rhett discovered Bonnet refitting the *Royal James* in the Cape Fear River. Bonnet hurriedly tried to sail downriver to the open sea, but the *Henry* intervened and was able to maneuver the *Royal James* onto a shoal. In the process, both the *Henry* and *Sea Nymph* ran aground as well; however, the *Henry* was within firing range of the *Royal James* and, as the tide gradually came in, the two ships fought fiercely for two hours with cannons booming and muskets blazing. Rhett's ships floated free first and they moved into position. The Charles Town men stormed the *Royal James* and overpowered Bonnet and his crew of thirty-five.

The pirates were returned to Charles Town and imprisoned in the bastion guardhouse (in the Provost Dungeon beneath the Old

Exchange Building). Bonnet was almost immediately greeted by a group of prominent gentlemen, those same scoundrels who had profited from their secret dealings with the pirate. They feared that if the pirate appeared before a judge the facts of their business relationship would be revealed. Public reaction would be strong against them. Bonnet's friends arranged to have the Gentleman Pirate placed under house arrest, and along with his lieutenant, David Herriot, the dandy was quartered at the mansion of the town marshal.

The sentries guarding the house were bribed and in the middle of the night, Bonnet and Herriot escaped, with Bonnet disguised as a woman. They used a small boat supplied by a sympathizer to escape to Sullivan's Island. The next morning their absence was discovered and Colonel Rhett formed a posse to re-capture Bonnet.

By the end of that first day, Rhett and a group of fifteen men located the pirate's hideout on Sullivan's Island. Herriot was killed during the skirmish and Bonnet surrendered, still wearing a dress. The Gentleman Pirate was shackled in the dungeon the night before his crew was marched to the gallows at White Point Gardens.

Bonnet was brought to trial in front of Justice Nicholas Trott's court. Bonnet pleaded his case, but was sentenced to be hanged. He sent urgent pleas to the governor to repeal the sentence. Several townspeople came forward to ask for his pardon, but Governor Johnson was unmoved by their pleas.

On December 10, 1718, Stede Bonnet was hanged at White Point Gardens, weeping on the gallows. His body dangled for several days before it was dumped into the low-tide mud. Today, a marker at White Point Gardens memorializes the event and the location of the executions.

He never disclosed the real reason he became a pirate.

After deserting Bonnet's crew Blackbeard headed for Teach's Hole. He stayed in hiding for several weeks waiting for the outrage of his Charles Town blockade to blow over, but by the fall of 1718, he was ready for action.

He left Bath, North Carolina, and almost immediately encountered two Virginia-bound French merchant ships laden with sugar and cocoa. Blackbeard seized the ships and transferred all the cargo onto one ship. He put the French crew on the other vessel and sent them back home. He then escorted the first French ship back to North Carolina and told the authorities an amazing tale. He claimed he had discovered the ship floating in the water, deserted by the crew. Realizing the value of the cargo, Governor Charles Eden and Customs Collector Tobias Knight chose to believe the story and the three split the booty.

To celebrate his grand fortune, Blackbeard headed to Ocracoke Island. The *Queen Anne's Revenge* was laden with food, rum and women picked up from the waterfront. Other notorious pirates, like Calico Jack Rackham and Charles Vane, arrived at Ocracoke with more women and rum. It soon became a huge, continual party that has become known as the "Ocracoke Orgy." Hundreds of pirates spent several weeks on the island drinking, eating and whoring with more than fifty wenches.

Word began to spread among the Outer Banks citizens about the presence of so many pirates. A panic spread along the Atlantic seaboard that Ocracoke Island was going to replace the Bahamas as the new pirate headquarters.

When Virginia Governor Alexander Spotswood was informed of Blackbeard's Charles Town blockade and the taking of the Virginia-bound French ships, he declared that he would not honor any pardon given to Blackbeard. Spotswood's political career was on the slide, and he believed that if he could get rid of the infamous Blackbeard, he would be a hero. Spotswood obtained two sloops (the *Jane* and the *Ranger*) and convinced the Royal Navy to supply the manpower, under the command of the oldest lieutenant in the navy, Lieutenant Robert Maynard. Maynard was promised a reward of one hundred pounds to bring back Blackbeard—dead or alive. Capturing Blackbeard would be a feather in his cap, and a route to a much-needed promotion. The biggest obstacle he faced was how to pinpoint the location of Teach's Hole. The problem was solved due to a lucky break—the arrest of Blackbeard's former quartermaster. Using torture, Maynard discovered the location of Teach's Hole.

Blackbeard enjoyed the orgy on Ocracoke so much that after it was over, he decided to extend the pleasure for his crew. Oblivious to the political winds blowing against him, and unaware of the executions of Bonnet and crew in Charles Town, Blackbeard left Ocracoke and headed to Teach's Hole with rum and women on board.

About the same time, Lieutenant Maynard set out from Virginia with fifty-eight men on two ships. They arrived at the inlet at dusk and spent a long night preparing for battle, waiting for dawn to navigate the inlet safely. Blackbeard and his men spent the night drinking and partying. In fact, most of the pirates were still drunk when the sails of Maynard's vessels became visible on the morning of November 21, 1718.

Maynard approached the Hole but, unfamiliar with the treacherous water, his two sloops ran aground on a sandbar. The pirate crew scrambled from their drinks and their women and hastily prepared for battle. While Maynard was stranded on the sandbar, Blackbeard took the opportunity to launch a full-scale assault. The half-hour battle resulted in ten dead pirates, and nine wounded. Maynard lost ten men and twenty-four were injured.

The highlight of the battle was a ten-minute duel between Blackbeard and Maynard. Blackbeard suffered five pistol wounds and twenty sword slashes before he collapsed on deck. The pirate was beheaded while he was still alive. Maynard returned to Virginia with the pirate's head dangling from the mast. Blackbeard's body was stripped of flesh and hung from a pole at the mouth of the Hampton River.

The death of Blackbeard marked the beginning of the end of the golden age of piracy along the Atlantic seaboard.

## The Odder Couple: Anne Bonny and Mark Read

Anne Cormac was born in Ireland in 1697, the result of an adulterous affair between her father, William Cormac, and his maid, Mary Brennan. Cormac was a successful barrister but due to the scandal, he was forced to leave Ireland. He and Mary brought the infant to Charles Town, South Carolina. William purchased a plantation and within a decade became a prosperous and respectable citizen.

Anne grew up a tomboy. She was described as "a strapping, boisterous girl of a fierce and courageous temper" with rowdy habits and short red hair. As a teenager she got into an argument with her English servant-maid and attacked her with a knife. Anne had to be restrained by her father. Other than her violent temper, Anne was considered a good and dutiful daughter. Until she reached age sixteen.

Anne began hanging out along the waterfront of Charles Town, each night hooking up with a different sailor or buccaneer. She became a familiar figure in the taverns along Bay Street and in the bawdy houses on Elliott Street. She was known for drinking, cursing and fighting as well as a man. One of her suitors ended up in the hospital when she beat him with a chair. She eventually married Jack Bonny, a sailor and sometime pirate.

Jack had more designs on Anne's money than Anne herself. As soon as her father learned of the marriage, he disinherited her. Furious, Anne attacked her father with an axe handle and burned down the family plantation. She and her husband then fled to the British–controlled port of New Providence (modern day Nassau, Bahamas).

Upon her arrival at New Providence, Anne immediately established her reputation. As she disembarked, a one-eared drunken sailor blocked her way and asked how much she would charge for an hour in bed. Anne responded by whipping out a pistol and shooting off his other ear. Within a week she was sharing a bed with the pirate Captain Jennings and his mistress, Meg. Anne also became the mistress of Chidley Bayard, the wealthiest man on the island. She was often seen in the company of Calico Jack Rackham, a pirate famous for his colorful manner of dress.

Another of Anne's friends was the homosexual Pierre Bouspeut (sometimes referred to as "Pierre the Pansy Pirate"). Pierre was a designer of fine velvet and silk clothing. He also ran a coffee house and dressmaking shop. Anne and Pierre learned that a French vessel was scheduled to arrive in port. The vessel was richly laden with costly fabrics. Together Anne and Pierre organized their first "privateering" raid.

With the aid of some of their pirate friends, including Calico Jack, they stole a boat from the abandoned wrecks in the harbor. They covered the topsail and deck with animal blood, and then coated themselves. In the bow they placed one of Pierre's dressmaker's dummies, dressed in women's clothing and splashed with blood. Anne stood on deck, hovering over this nightmarish figure with a blood-soaked axe, and under a full moon they sailed out to the French vessel. When the French crew caught sight of this demonic ship, covered in a sickly sheen illuminated by the light of the moon, they were so horrified by the impending mayhem that they turned over the cargo without a fight.

At this time, the British government sought to reestablish its power and jurisdiction over Jamaica. Captain Woodes Rogers offered the king's pardon to all pirates who would turn themselves in and offer to reform. Anne refused, knowing that she could not be pardoned for the attempted murder of her father. She, with Calico Jack, Pierre and a group of unrepentant buccaneers, broke through a blockade that Rogers had positioned in the harbor. As they sailed past the blockade, Anne stood on deck, stripped to the waist like an Amazon, dressed in black velvet trousers designed by Pierre. With one hand resting on the hilt of her sword, and the other waving a long silk scarf at the astonished governor, she sailed past "as daintily as any fine lady being seen off on a long ocean voyage."

Anne quickly established her position aboard this ship by shooting a sailor who tried to force himself on her sexually. Officially she was second in command; however, within a few days, she had thrown Calico Jack out of the captain's quarters and resided there alone.

They dropped off their pirate crew at the next port, and hired a new crew. Even though the crew was hired under the guise that Jack was in charge, they learned quickly that the "captain's wench" was no typical woman. Anne was in charge. Calico Jack was on board as Anne's second in command, and her sometime partner in the captain's bed. Anne immersed herself in the pirate culture, becoming as savage as any of the male crew. She and Calico Jack prowled the shipping lanes around Jamaica, plundering ships and taking as prisoners those they didn't kill.

One such prisoner was a handsome man named Mark Read, who was captured on a Dutch sloop. Mark caught Anne's eye. Soon, Mark Read was spending his nights in the captain's cabin. This intimacy aroused the jealousy of Calico Jack. He once threatened to slit Mark's throat, but Anne responded, "If you do, you'll answer to me." Calico knew better than to battle Anne one-on-one, so he backed down.

However, one night, as Jack listened to the sounds of sex emanating from behind the captain's door, he could no longer control his jealousy. He burst through the cabin door with a knife in his hand and murder in his heart. He discovered two naked women stretched out on the bed together. Mark Read was actually a woman, named Mary Read!

Mary Read was much older than Anne. She was born in the mid-1670s in London to a prosperous family. The Read family practiced the paternal system of primogeniture—only the firstborn male child may inherit the family name and wealth. Soon after Mary's birth, her father and brother died and her mother began to raise Mary as a boy, changing her daughter's name to Mark.

The ruse worked for a time. The grandparents continued to supply the family with money until Mark became a teenager. It became more difficult to pass Mary off as a male, particularly when Mary seduced a young man in their social circle. Mary and her mother were banished from the family.

Mary ran away, and continued to play the role of a male. She became a soldier in the English army, where she fell in love with an infantryman. Together they left the army and in 1697 opened a tavern called The Three Horseshoes, right about the time her future lover and comrade-in-arms Anne Bonny was born in Ireland. Mary ran the tavern for sixteen years with her husband until he died, leaving her alone once again. In order to survive, Mary took up her old habit. She slipped into her Mark Read role and became a shipmate on a Dutch sloop bound for the West Indies. However, before they arrived in Jamaica, pirates captured the sloop. Mark Read was given a choice: join the sweet trade or die. Mark Read became part of the pirate crew of Anne Bonny and Calico Jack.

Even after the discovery of "Mark's" true gender, Anne and Mary (as she now called herself) remained a couple. They both alternately donned male and female clothing, as the situation warranted. They built their pirate fleet up to three ships, and soon abandoned all caution, ruthlessly plundering ships.

They raided a ship called the *Royal Queen*, owned by Anne's former lover, Chidley Bayard. They took the *Royal Queen* not by force, but by subterfuge and sex. Anne seduced Captain Hudson into bringing her aboard the *Royal Queen*. She drugged his wine, and then took him to bed. After he was unconscious, Anne secretly doused the firing pins of the ship's cannons with water. She left the captain asleep the next morning, but returned that night with her three ships. The *Royal Queen*'s gunmen were unable to open fire and they were easily captured. The only death was Captain Hudson, whose throat was slashed by the jealous Mary Read.

Soon, a British man-of-war was sent to capture "those infamous women." In October 1720, the pirates were taken by surprise. In a panic, Calico Jack and all twelve of the men in the crew ran below deck to hide in the cargo hold. Only Anne and Mary remained topside to defend the ship. They were quickly overwhelmed. Mary, so angry at her shipmates' cowardice, shouted into the hold for them to "come up and fight like a man." But no one came. Mary fired her pistols into the hold several times, killing one pirate and wounding several others.

The women surrendered, and the pirate crew was taken to St. Jago de la Vega, Jamaica, where separate trials were scheduled for the men and women. On November 17, 1720, Calico Jack and the rest of the men were convicted of piracy. The governor of Jamaica sentenced them to be hanged.

Anne and Mary were allowed to visit Calico Jack on the night before his execution. Anne told him, "If you had fought like a man, you wouldn't have to be hanged like a dog."

The trial of the women took place on November 28. They were accused of piracy and attacking seven ships. They both pleaded "not guilty," but they were convicted and sentenced to death by hanging. When the governor asked the condemned if they had anything to say, Anne and Mary promptly said: "Sir, we plead our bellies," meaning they were pregnant. This was a common plea for women sentenced to death, the point being that no court would hang an innocent, albeit unborn, life.

After an examination, they were both found to be pregnant, (by whom no one ever determined, though Calico Jack seems to be the best candidate) and they escaped the death penalty. Mary contracted a violent fever in prison and died. She was buried on April 28, 1721, in Jamaica.

Most records indicate that Anne Bonny was paroled by her father. She returned to Charles Town, where she married a local businessman named James Burleigh, and gave birth to eight children with him. Anne died in Charleston in 1782 at the age of eighty-four.

*Author's Note: It is estimated that there were more than three thousand pirates operating in the Caribbean and off the eastern Atlantic coast around 1720. Anne Bonny and Mary Read are the only women documented to have entered this ultra male world disguised as men. The fact that they both ended up on the same ship and became lesbian lovers has to rank as among the odder facts of history.*

# America's First Free Love Religious Cult: 1724

The Dutartre family was descended from French Huguenot refugees who fled to Carolina after King Louis XIV revoked the Edict of Nantes in 1685. The edict, invoked by King Henry IV, forbade the slaughter of Protestants by Catholics. Once Louis XIV revoked the edict, Protestants once again became fair game. They fled Europe by the thousands, many arriving in Charles Town from 1685 to 1720.

The fourteen members of the Dutartre family (father, mother, four brothers and four sisters, plus spouses) lived in the Orange Quarter (present-day area of Orange, Tradd and Legare Streets), where they struggled to survive as poor dirt farmers. In 1722, a Moravian minister from Switzerland named Christian George arrived in Charles Town with his friend Peter Rombert.

Rombert quickly married one of the widowed Dutartre women. Within a year George and Rombert had convinced the Dutartres that they were the only family on earth who possessed knowledge of the one true God. The family withdrew from public worship and refused to speak or interact with anyone outside the family circle.

This began their legal troubles with authorities. The family claimed God ordered them to bear no arms and, therefore, they refused to comply with the militia law, which stated that every man older than seventeen be armed and part of the local militia. They would not pay their taxes, nor do their part in repairing and maintaining highways. Finally the local justice of the peace, Captain Simmons, issued warrants against them.

By this time Rombert and George had weaved more of their religious magic; they convinced the family that God had revealed Himself to them in visions to Rombert, who assumed the role of prophet for the group.

Rombert told the Dutartres that the world was so wicked that God was going to destroy everything and everyone. Only one family would be spared to repopulate the earth. Rombert told them that the Dutartres had been chosen to be the next Adam and Eve, the next Noah.

Rombert ordered them to construct a compound with a ten-foot log wall. He postulated that when the "others" realized only the Dutartres would be spared, there would be retribution. They must be prepared to protect themselves from the mob.

Then Rombert dropped the big one. He told the family that God had ordered him to begin the repopulation effort. To accomplish that, he and George must sleep with each of the Dutartre women. If they were not successful in planting their seed, it was God's will that each male should sleep with each female in the family until such time that each woman was with child. Rombert assured them that God would not consider it a sin for brother to be with sister, father to be with daughter or mother to be with son. The Dutartres were doing God's work. Rombert also convinced them that every member of the family would be resurrected in the aftermath of God's destruction.

Within several weeks, the youngest Dutartre female, Judith, was pregnant; by whom no one could say. When the acts of incest and adultery were finally discovered, the community was shocked and outraged. Captain Simmons was forced to issue a warrant, which bound Judith over to the general sessions court for violating the statute against bastardy.

The constable who was serving the warrant suspected trouble, so he arrived with a group of five men. The family was on the watch behind their compound wall and announced to Rombert the arrival of the group. Rombert assured them it was God's command to defend themselves. So the family, who first refused to comply with the militia act because God ordered them to bear no arms, now armed themselves against the Charles Town authorities. Their prophet Rombert assured them that no weapon could harm them.

The family fired at the constable, who immediately retreated back to Charles Town. Captain Simmons gathered the militia and later in the day approached the compound. The family opened fire, and Simmons was shot dead. The militia returned fire, killing one of the women in the house, and then, by sheer force, the militia stormed the compound and arrested seven inhabitants.

Four of the family males were tried in general sessions court in Charles Town in September 1724: Peter Dutartre, the father; Peter Rombert, the prophet; Michael Boneau, husband of a Dutartre woman; and Christian George, the minister.

During the trial, the men appeared to be unconcerned about the crimes they had committed or their fate. They were convinced that God was on their side and even if they were executed, they, just like Jesus, would be resurrected on the third day.

They were marched to the gallows near the public market (present-day location of City Hall). Standing with ropes around their necks the condemned men confidently told the gathered crowd they would soon see them again. They were hanged together and their bodies were allowed to dangle from the gallows for several days—so the resurrection (or lack thereof) could be witnessed by the public.

Judith Dutartre and her two brothers, David and John, aged eighteen and twenty, were the three other prisoners. Judith, due to her pregnancy, was not tried. David and John were convicted and condemned to prison. They were sullen and arrogant, confident God would protect them. However, after the third day of their kinfolk's execution (and the fourth, and fifth), when none of the men hanging from the gallows was resurrected, David and John began to see the error of their ways. They later asked for a pardon from the court, which they received.

Less than five months later, David Dutartre attacked and murdered a stranger on the street. He was brought to trial and told the court he killed the man because God commanded him to do so. David was sentenced to death.

A total of seven people (two innocents) died as a result of what has to be one of the most unusual cases of religious fanaticism in American history ever to be recorded.

# Chapter Three
# The Holy City

*They are devoted to debauchery and probably carry it to a greater length than any other people.*

Josiah Quincy, of Boston, commenting after his visit to Charles Town

## Marching Toward Freedom—The Stono Rebellion

Many of the slaves working on Lowcountry rice plantations were educated and well trained. In Africa they had been kings and princes, but on these remote American plantations, they ranked little higher than a mule in importance to their owner. The rice plantations were sprawling remote places, some of them more than ten thousand acres, large enough so that the majority of plantation slaves had little interaction with their white masters.

Some slaves had a great deal of contact with Spanish Jesuits from St. Augustine, who conducted secret missionary trips into the slave territory of Georgia and South Carolina. They told stories of small groups of runaway slaves who successfully made their way from South Carolina to Florida, and were given their freedom and land by the Spanish authorities.

In 1720, the first serious slave conspiracy was uncovered and all of the blacks involved were "burnt, hang'd or banish'd." At that time Negroes outnumbered whites 39,000 to 20,000 in Carolina; a prospect that made many whites uneasy. New powers were given to the night watch to prevent slave uprisings. A well-armed, forty-eight-member force was to patrol the streets nightly to "Quell any Designs by Negroes." Any black who refused to stop when so ordered could be shot. Members of the watch became emboldened with their power and often became as much of a problem as the criminals.

In mid-August 1739, a Charles Town newspaper announced the Security Act, a response to whites' fears of insurrection. The act required all white men to carry firearms to church on Sundays. Anyone who didn't comply with the new law by September 29 would be subjected to a fine. The paper also announced a debate over a stricter "Negro Act" to place more restrictions on the movements of slaves.

Unfortunately, these measures did not stop a group of about twenty slaves who gathered early on the moring of September 9, 1739, near the Stono River in St. Paul's Parish, less than twenty miles from Charles Town. The slaves attacked a shop that sold firearms and ammunition, killing the two shopkeepers. The slaves then armed themselves and walked to the house of Mr. Godfrey, where they killed him, his son and daughter and then burned the house. After that, the mob headed south toward Florida.

They reached Wallace's Tavern (in present-day Ravenel, South Carolina) at dawn. Because the innkeeper had a reputation as being kind to his slaves, his life was spared. The white inhabitants of the next six houses were not so lucky and all were killed. The slaves that belonged to Thomas Rose successfully hid their master, but they were forced to join the rebellion. Other (most) slaves willingly joined the rebellion. By eleven in the morning the group was about fifty strong, armed with rifles, pistols and farm implements. The few whites they now encountered were chased down and killed. The one who got away was Lieutenant Governor William Bull, on horseback. He escaped from the mob and galloped to spread the alarm.

According to one account, that evening "they halted in a field and set to dancing, Singing and beating Drums to draw more Negroes to them." In less than twenty-four hours they had grown into a mob of "above sixty, some say a hundred," marched ten miles and killed at least twenty-five whites.

Monday afternoon more than one hundred white men set out in armed pursuit. They reached the slaves' encampment at dusk. When they approached, the slaves fired two shots and the whites returned fire with a deluge of bullets, killing fourteen slaves immediately. By dark, twenty whites were dead; thirty slaves were killed and thirty more had escaped. Most were captured over the next few days. The whites "cutt off their heads and set them up at every mile post they came to."

The council had been debating a Negro Act. After the Stono Rebellion they stopped debating and quickly approved the act. Slaves would no longer be allowed to travel without written permission. They could not assemble in groups without the presence of whites. They were forbidden to raise their own food, possess money or learn to read. The use of drums, horns and other "loud instruments" that might be used by slaves to communicate with each other was forbidden. Some of these restrictions had been in effect before the Negro Act, but now they were strictly enforced. The punishment for a minor offense was death—hanging followed by decapitation, or being burned alive.

## Society for the Propagation of the Gospel

Around 1700 a religious movement started in England. The goal was to bring all Protestant denominations within the liturgy of the Church of England. The Society for the Propagation of the Gospel in Foreign Parts (SPG) was founded in 1701. It provided funds for libraries and missionaries.

In Charles Town, there was a strong coalition of public men who supported the goals of the SPG. The coalition included Governor Nathaniel Johnson, Chief Justice Nicholas Trott and Reverend Gideon Johnson (who was fond of Madeira). These men were dedicated and influential, but the tide of debauchery was strong against them. Many of the locals were just as dedicated to different goals—drinking and wenching. Many were appalled.

Margaret Kennett, Charles Town's first businesswoman, commented that the locals are "Trained in Luxury and are the Greatest Debauchers in Nature." The Reverend Levi Durand stated, "this country is more infested with free thinkers than it is with enthusiasts [Christians]." Josiah Quincy of Boston was astounded by the behavior of the citizens. He wrote: "They are devoted to debauchery and probably carry it to a greater length than any other people."

By 1720, Charles Town was one of the busiest ports in the colonies. The harbor hosted an average of one hundred fifty ships per day. Each ship carried a crew of at least a dozen, with some carrying a crew of more than fifty. A conservative estimate would place about eighteen hundred sailors from a dozen foreign ports taking their liberties in Charles Town at one time. After months at sea, these sailors would arrive in port and they wanted three things: wine, women and song, not always in that order.

A tax on rum was imposed in 1720 to pay for the building of the new St. Philip's Church. Bawdy houses like The Bear and other grog shops near Roper's Alley and Beresford Alley (Chalmers Street) offered drink, entertainment and sex. Punch houses like the Two Brewers on Church Street and the Pig and Whistle on Tradd Street served sailors, wenches and locals. They served rum-based "slings," "flipps" and "toddies."

The Act of 1721 made the courts the guardians of community morals. The ministers needed help. In fact, ministers of every denomination except Methodists drank for pleasure. The court had full power "to license all taverns, victualling houses, ale houses, punch houses and public inns." Any tavern "convicted of being disorderly, as entertaining of servants, Negroes, common drunkards, lewd and idle and disorderly persons, selling liquors on Sundays, or times of Divine service" were to be suppressed by the courts. A fine of twenty pounds was levied on any tavern operating without a license. Justices could compel disorderly and idle persons to find useful employment or imprison them.

The courts were empowered to punish drunkards, Sabbath-breakers and profane cursers. They were "to suppress all vice and immorality within their respective jurisdictions." Courts were described as "the Justice sitting in his chair—many in the Crowd...Cursing and Swearing... others intoxicated with Liquor."

In 1763, sixty-six tavern licenses were issued. Five years later the number had doubled—approximately one tavern for every five adult males. Half the licenses were issued to women. It was illegal for artisans to operate a drinking establishment, so most dodged the law by having their wives obtain the licenses. Most of the taverns doubled as brothels; alcohol on the first floor, flesh on the upper floors.

For the affluent, the most popular house was Charles Shepheard's tavern at the northeast corner of Church and Broad Streets (46 Broad Street). Another hot spot was Thomas Nightingale's house just outside the city, which had a bowling alley.

The Sign of Bacchus was located on Bay Street and operated by Benjamin and Catherine Backhouse. Backhouse was a blacksmith, and Catherine owned the tavern license. It featured a dining room, a long room, a front room, piazza and cellar and was furnished with mahogany furniture by noted craftsman Thomas Elfe. There were nineteen beds for lodging and a bathtub. Bacchus employed eighteen slaves and an Irish indentured servant.

As the rowdiness of the nightlife spiraled out of control, robberies and violence in Charles Town increased. Citizens complained about the "notorious neglect" of the Night Watch. (Some things never change—citizens have always complained about corruption among the police force.) An investigation discovered the Night Watch was found to lack "men of good character" and that while on duty more than thirty of the Night Watch sold "Juggs of Liquor to Seaman and Negroes."

Most egregious to the clergy and council members was that during the Sabbath, "low houses" continued to do a booming business. The council sought to remedy the problem by issuing orders to apprehend on Sunday "all Loose and Idle Persons going a Pleasuring during the Time of Divine Service." However, the people revolted against what they called "military rule" and the order was revoked.

In 1720 the Reverend Doctor Alexander Garden was appointed as commissary and to the pulpit of St. Philip's. He was endowed with legal powers to conduct ecclesiastical courts for the purpose of trying errant ministers. The job he faced in Charles Town was monumental. The SPG was responsible for sending most of the clergy to Carolina and the Anglican Church was disliked by the poor and uneducated due to their condescending attitude. Most of Garden's parish, however, consisted of the Anglican elite, and he had his concerns about the gentry. The Charles Town elite was so wealthy; they felt no need to work. Garden was shocked by their lack of intellectual curiosity. He noted they were "absolutely above every occupation but eating, drinking, lolling, smoking and sleeping."

In addition to the attitude of the parishioners, Garden had to deal with wayward members of the clergy. SPG missionaries constituted 69 percent of the unworthy clerics in the colony. Reverend Brian Hunt (SPG) of St. John's parish fell into debt. He was accused of drunkenness, abusive language and lying. To raise money to satisfy his debts, Hunt began marrying the couples no other clergy would join. In 1727, against the wishes of her guardians, he married a young teenager, Miss Gibbon Cawood, to Robert Wright in a secret midnight ceremony. Garden and other ministers condemned the wedding. Hunt was jailed in Charles Town, resigned his parish and returned to England.

Another of the nine disgraced ministers was Reverend John Winteley (SPG). In the fall of 1728, he was forcibly restrained by his Christ Church parishioners (in present-day Mt. Pleasant) from entering the pulpit. Labeled a "whore monger and drunkard," he was dismissed as minister by Reverend Garden. Winteley took up residence in Charles Town where he was often seen in taverns and walking the streets "much in Liquor." Winteley made "lewd attempts" on six women. Reverend Garden finally used his power to have Winteley removed from the colony altogether. John Fulton succeeded Winteley at the Christ Church parish. Fulton was also removed by Garden for "habitual drunkenness."

Edward Dyson (SPG) served briefly in a local parish before leaving. Garden called Dyson a "notorious drunkard."

In 1734, Laurence O'Neill (SPG) enjoyed a short career as a clergyman, until his arrest for "bastardy and public lewdness."

Stephen Roe (SPG) of St. George's Parish, 1737–42, left a wife back in England, but upon arrival in Charles Town he claimed bachelorhood. He courted the daughter of a prominent parishioner. He was transferred to Boston where he fathered a child with his landlady's daughter.

Also dismissed was Michael Smith, an Irish cleric, who traveled about the Lowcountry with a woman he claimed to be his nurse, but she also shared his bed. Smith was married, but while his wife was lying in bed with a serious illness he was traveling with his "nurse."

William Peaseley (SPG) was dismissed from his parish for "visiting a woman frequently and at late hours."

During late 1739 and into 1740, a religious revival swept across the American colonies—the "Great Awakening." Leading the charge in

America was the Reverend George Whitefield, an adherent to John Wesley's Methodism.

Methodism was a religion of daily emotional experience, involving soul and body. Most Methodists were women, common whites and slaves. Few white gentlemen were converts. Methodism presented a distinct worship style that differed from other Protestants, especially Anglicans, from which Methodism sprang. Methodists revolted against the "formal" or cold act of worship. They were, however, considered dour and somber, with an aversion to pleasure. They reveled in emotion, zeal and bliss in their relations with God. Methodists abstained from drink, dance and gaming. They shut off all worldly enjoyment and in replacement they searched for spiritual ecstasy. Methodists were not popular among the elite in Charles Town. One of the Methodist clergy was nearly drowned in a public horse trough.

Whitefield mesmerized the city with his passionate preaching, whipping his congregation into a fever pitch. Whitefield preached for hours against high living and ostentatious displays. He held services at the Congregational Church and the French Huguenot Church and from the pulpit he declared war on the Anglican Church. He said the Anglican clergy were so preoccupied with their own material wealth, they had allowed their congregations to go astray. He castigated them for failing to teach slaves Christianity.

Dr. Garden stated that only a "lower sort" attended Whitefield's services. He called the Methodist a "pig, and preacher of Gibberish." One of Whitefield's "lower sort" converts was Mrs. Anne Le Brasseur, a wealthy, twice-widowed lady. She dressed extravagantly and lived a lavish lifestyle—everything Whitefield abhorred. In fact, during one of his lectures he pointed to Mrs. Le Brasseur as an example of how not to dress. The public humiliation was so great that after the service the lady returned home and killed herself with a pistol.

Hugh Bryan was one of Reverend Whitefield's most passionate converts. At forty-one years of age, he was deeply disturbed by the death of his young wife and he focused all his energy toward his religious zeal. He viewed the great fire that ravaged Charles Town in 1740 as condemnation of the Anglican Church. In a letter published January 8, 1741, in the *South Carolina Gazette,* Bryan and Whitefield claimed the fire as a part of God's wrath against the Church. The fire joined droughts, plagues and other natural disasters as signs of God's displeasure with the Church or, as Bryan called them, "wayward people." Bryan called priests "thieves and robbers" who "did not follow the Foot-steps of our true Shepherd, but coveted the Fleece only." Whitefield was imprisoned for libeling the Anglican Church. He soon raised bail and departed for England.

Bryan believed the divine spirit guided him and it was feared that he was organizing a slave insurrection. In 1741 neighbors began to complain to authorities of the "great assemblies of Negroes" on Bryan's property. In the evenings he was preaching to large gatherings of slaves. During one of his "religious trances" the spirit supposedly revealed to Bryan that in April 1742 a successful slave insurrection would be "the Destruction of Charles Town...executed by Negroes with fire and sword." Bryan publicized his vision to warn the white population of the consequences of their sins. Bryan also attempted, guided by the spirit, to part the waters of the Atlantic Ocean like Moses, with just a wand. His slaves were to follow him back to Africa. When that failed, he claimed he would be able to walk across water. He became the laughing stock of the city, but due to his opinion against slavery he was considered to be dangerous and was taken seriously.

Bryan was arrested for assembling blacks. While in prison, he began to see the folly of his ways. He wrote a letter to the governor claiming he believed his spirit guide had not been God, but Satan. He claimed it had all been a "delusion of Satan." Charges were dropped and Bryan returned to his plantation to live a quiet life as a planter.

The Reverend Levi Durand wrote in 1744, "This country [Charleston] is more infested with free thinkers than it is with enthusiasts [passionate Christians]." Durand was appalled at "this province, where infidelity, profaneness, heresy, blasphemy and the most offensive breaches of common morality have scarce ever appeared with more insolence."

During the 1760s there was a dramatic increase in "notorious bawds and strumpets and idle persons roaming the streets, swearing and talking obscenely." Mary McDowell and Mary Grant of Pinckney Street were cited for keeping "a most notorious brothel" and for "harboring loose and idle women." The assembly criticized the "superabundance of licensed Taverns and Tippling Houses, gaming houses and disorderly houses."

The Reverend Charles Woodmason wrote extensively about the behavior of citizens, claiming "The Open profanation of the Lords Day in this Province is one of the most crying Sins in it—and is carried to a great height—among the low Class, it is abus'd by women frolicking and Wantoness. By others in Drinking Bouts and Card Playing—Even in and about Charles Town, the Taverns have more visitants than the Churches."

Woodmason was also concerned about the sexual behavior of his congregation. He complained of "promiscuous cohabiting" and people being "Addicted to those practices which would naturally produce Children." He often traveled as an itinerant minister, traveling the back woods of the Lowcountry, trying to convert dissenters (Baptists and Presbyterians) to Anglicism. He wrote:

> *This Day we had another Specimen of the...Temper of the Presbyterians. They gave away 2 Barrels of Whisky to the Populace to make drink... to disturb the Service —The Company got drunk by 10 oth Clock and we could hear them hooping, and hallowing like Indians...They are the lowest Pack of Wretches my Eyes ever saw...How would the Polite People of London stare, to see the Females (many very pretty) come to service...in a short petticoat only, barefooted and Bare Legged...Quite in a state of Nature for Nakedness is counted for nothing.*
>
> *They delight in their present low, lazy sluttish, heathenish, hellish Life and seem not desirous of changing it. Both Men and Women will do any thing to come at Liquor. They will commit the grossiest Enormities...and laugh at all Admonition.*

The Baptists, in particular, did not like Woodmason trying to convert them to Anglicanism. They called Woodmason a Jesuit—Catholicism being the one religion not tolerated in Carolina at that time. He would conduct public services in the evening and spend the night in a local house. One night, while asleep, someone stole his clergyman's robe and put it on. The man then visited a brothel, sleeping with several of the girls while dressed in the cleric's robe. The next day, the girls all publicly claimed to have been visited that night by the parson.

Some jottings from Woodmason's journal describe the conditions and situations he endured:

> *Many hundreds live in Concubinage—swopping their Wives as Cattel.*
>
> *The Schoolmaster...having been drunk for some days past—gave me such horrid abuse...I should have caned Him—and was about to whip a Stumpet whom he keeps for her Lewdness and Prophanness—*

*but was prevented...there is a Magistrate here but he is Presbyterian... Instead of punishing these worthless Sinners he protects them.*

*Married some Whores and Rogues (Gratis). After Service they went to Revelling Drinking Singing Dancing and Whoring—and most of the Company were drunk before I quitted the Spot...their Dresses almost as loose and Naked as the Indians.*

*Adultery and Fornication are gloried in and practiced in open Noon Day. Gaming and Gambling—Rioting and Drunkenness—Gambling and Wagering—Fighting and Brawling take up most of your Time and Attention.*

On the influence of taverns affecting church attendance:

*It tends to all Kinds of Debauchery: For of those who may quit the Tavern and return home, they are so heavy, sleepy drunk and stupid, as to be unable, utterly unfit to attend Public Worship on Sunday.*

On the style of worship he encountered:

*And as for Hymns. We do not disallow of them, provided they be Solemn, Sublime, Elegant and Devout...*[but] *these Singing Matches lie under the Imputation of being only Rendezvous of Idlers, under the Mask of Devotion, Meetings for Young Persons to carry on Intrigues and Amours...of both sexes to make Assignations. On half of those who resort to...Assemblies go more for the sake of Liquor, than Instruction or Devotion.*

*As for Adulteries, the present State of most Persons around 9/10 of whom now labour under a filthy Distemper (as is well known to all)...and nothing more leads to this that what they call their Love Feasts and Kiss of Charity. To which Feasts, celebrated at Night, much Liquor is privately carried and deposited on the Roads, in Bye Paths and Places. The Assignations made on Sundays at the Singing Clubs...it is no wonder That things are as they are when many Young Persons have 3, 4, 5, 6, miles to walk home in the dark Night...or staying perhaps all Night at some Cabbin and sleeping together either doubly or promiscuously? Or a girl being mounted behind.*

On the ineffectiveness of local ministers:

> *Is there not one less Hogshead of Liquor less consum'd...or any tavern shut up—so far from it, that there has been Great Increase of Both. Are Riots, Frolics, Races, Games, Cards, Dice, Dances less frequent now than formerly? Are fewer persons to be seen in Taverns? Or reeling or drunk on the roads? Have any of the Storekeepers given up their Licences, or refus'd to retail Poison? Are there fewer Bastards born? Are more Girls with their Virginity about them? There are rather more Bastards, more Mullatoes born than before. Out of 100 Women that I marry in a year...Six are without child.*

Woodmason also felt it necessary to preach a sermon titled "On Correct Behavior in Church." Part of the sermon were ten rules for attendance, which included: Be on time; do not spit tobacco, cough or chew; do not bring dogs to church; and do not drink in church.

You've got to love a city where the Christians have to be told not to drink in church.

The Anglican Church was active and dominant in Charleston. The other religions—the dissenters—scrambled to gather adherents, but they remained a decided minority well into the twentieth century. Why is that? Perhaps because the Methodists, Baptists, Lutherans and Presbyterians all decried the evils of alcohol and gambling. The Anglicans were more tolerant, much more tolerant. If you were Anglican, you could have your religion and your fun too.

## COLONIAL DEBAUCHERY

The incidence of sexual relations between white males and female black slaves occurred in all of Britain's North American colonies. In South Carolina it not only occurred, it was openly discussed and accepted. Several brothels offered only black women and catered exclusively to white males. That was just the tip of the iceberg. For every public mixed race relationship, there were a dozen more kept secret. Josiah Quincy of Boston was shocked at the casual way white men spoke of interracial affairs with "no reluctance...or shame."

The gentry became alarmed at the number of "disorderly" whites and slaves within the city. They believed that "tippling houses were the source from which many Evils...daily committed derive." They were alarmed that they could not depend on the Night Watch to control the "growing Vice and Immorality." Several men on the Night Watch ran "dram shops" and encouraged the sale of spirituous liquors to the "low and disorderly." Their wives operated the "house" on the second floor of the shop.

During the Revolutionary War the city's population swelled with more than two thousand soldiers and multi-national sailors. The soldiers and sailors thronged to the tippling houses along the waterfront where they gambled and drank and found "willing female companionship." A riot broke out between French and American sailors along Elliott Street that damaged more than a dozen structures and resulted in the arrest of more than forty persons.

Rumors were rampant that the British were trying to incite Indian attacks against the city and were planning slave insurrections across the state. Mounted militia patrolled the city twenty-four hours a day. Two local Loyalist merchants, Laughlin Martin and James Dealy, had celebrated the rumor that blacks, Catholics and Indians were being supplied arms by the British. Martin and Dealy were stripped naked "tarred, feathered and carted through the streets." A mob followed the cart, throwing rotted meat and fruit.

Fearing the black insurrection, the government ordered the imprisonment of blacks for suspicion of planning a riot. One of the blacks, Thomas Jeremiah, was a successful free black, owned property and "had several slaves of his own." The case against Jeremiah was based on testimony of two slaves, Sambo and Jemmy. Sambo claimed that Jeremiah had told him a "great war was coming to help the poor Negroes." On August 11, 1775, Jeremiah was found guilty of insurrection and sentenced "to be hanged, and then burned to ashes."

This incident only reinforced the white's convictions that a slave rebellion was imminent. Whites began to punish slaves for what were once considered minor offenses. A notice for the runaway slave named Limus was placed in the *Gazette* that read:

> *Limus is well known in Charles Town for his saucy and impudent tongue... he has the audacity to tell me he will be free, that he will serve no Man.*

The next day, a mob of four hundred seized a British soldier. He was tarred and feathered and paraded through town in a cart. Royal Governor

William Campbell was forced to flee the city and take refuge on a British warship, HMS *Tamar*, in the harbor.

During the entire period of the Revolutionary War (1775–1782), groups of mobs periodically roamed the city lynching Loyalists, Tories and blacks suspected of conspiracy. Any time a fire broke out in the city, blacks were rounded up and accused. Any person detected carrying away property not his own from the site of a fire was to be pilloried and "to have their ears cut off." Arsonists received the death penalty. Two "Negro wenches" were "tried and convicted" of willfully setting fires. Ironically they were burnt to death.

On the night of January 15, 1778, a fire began at the intersection of Queen and Union (now State) Streets. It burned all the way south to Tradd, destroying more than two hundred and fifty homes. The losses were more than three million dollars. Two British sympathizers were arrested and executed for the crime.

And then, the British laid siege to the city for forty-two days before marching into the city. They confiscated all munitions and arms in the city, storing them in the powder magazine on Magazine Street, between Archdale and Mazyk (now Logan) Streets. However, there was an accident inside the magazine and a "horrible explosion" occurred. There were some "sixty people...burnt beyond recognition, half-dead and writhing like worms." Mutilated bodies and limbs were hanging from trees and nearby houses.

General Sir Henry Clinton established his headquarters on King Street, in Miles Brewton's mansion. In fear of his soldier's safety, Clinton confined former patriot leaders to barracks. He promised a pardon for all "treasonable offenses" to citizens who took an oath of allegiance to the British government. Hundreds of runaway slaves flocked to the city to "join the King's army." Clinton feared the blacks might become dangerous to the city and ordered them to be confined in a "large sugar house" located somewhere near the present-day area of Queen and Logan Streets. The health of the slaves deteriorated in the sugar house and so many died that the "Negro burying ground" in Church Street became "so noxious" that the citizens complained.

However, Clinton's most effective decision, for the health and safety for his troops, was to arrest "dozens of infected women" and banish them from the city.

# Lowcountry Gullah and Root

The first importation of Africans into colonial America occurred in 1612 at Jamestown, Virginia. One hundred years later, Charles Town had become the center of North American slave trade.

The European castles that dotted the West African coastline during the seventeenth and eighteenth centuries were not grand and festive palaces. They were fortresses built by the Portuguese as trading centers. During the African slave trade, these castles became the places where African princes, princesses and peasants all shared the same fate behind the massive stone walls—bondage. Hundreds of thousands of Africans were crammed in dark, poorly ventilated cells, waiting to be loaded onto slave ships for the long and horrifying trip across the Atlantic Ocean.

These Africans were chained to strangers from other West African tribes, and became part of the Triangular Trade, or the Middle Passage. The Triangular Trade route began in the West Indies where ships were loaded with sugar and molasses. Those ships then sailed to Massachusetts and Charles Town, where the sugar and molasses were traded for rum, guns and cloth. These products were taken to West Africa where they were exchanged for Africans, who were subsequently taken to the West Indies (Barbados and Jamaica).

Once in the West Indies the slaves were "broken in" on the sugar plantations. They were beaten, denied food and humiliated until they appeared tame and obedient to the slave trader's demands. Then they were shipped to Charleston, Savannah, Norfolk or other slave-trading ports in America to be sold.

Frequently, slave ships were nothing more than converted cattle ships; they sailed with five hundred or more Africans aboard a ship designed for only two hundred. Men, women and children were packed in tiny compartments like chickens. They were often forced to sit or lie in their own urine, feces and vomit. Thousands of slaves became sick and died.

Conditions were so horrible that many African captives plotted with their shackled partners to commit suicide, preferring death to slavery. Suicide took many forms: jumping ship into shark-infested waters, open rebellion against captains and overseers and refusing to eat or drink.

An estimated twenty million Africans were shipped from the west coast of Africa. Because of the highly skilled nature of the residents who had been farmers, fishermen, miners and artisans, these slaves provided valuable labor for the booming and expanding rice, cotton and indigo plantations in America. The Africans who arrived in Charleston saw much that was familiar in terrain and weather.

Rice was a labor-intensive industry. The slaves from Madagascar had been harvesting rice for centuries and they soon became a sought-after commodity. By 1720, Africans in America outnumbered Europeans. By 1806, when federal law prohibited the slave trade, most historians agree that over 250,000 slaves had been imported into America, mostly through Charleston, Savannah and New Orleans. Today, 30 million living African Americans trace their ancestry to those 250,000 imported slaves.

According to the 1860 U.S. census, there were only eighty-eight slaveholders in the United States who owned more than three hundred slaves. Of that number, twenty-nine owned rice plantations in the Charleston area. Of the fourteen slaveholders who owned more than five hundred slaves, nine lived in Charleston. The slave population in Charleston was fourteen thousand. In Savannah there were eight thousand slaves, and in Richmond, Virginia, slaves numbered eleven thousand. Samuel Dyssli, a Swiss settler in Charles Town said, "Carolina looks more like a Negro country than like a country settled by white people. There are calculated to be always 20 blacks to one white man."

Slave culture of the Sea Islands was different from other slave cultures in the South. The tremendous size of the rice plantations demanded a huge amount of labor. The "task" system of dividing work among the slaves was created to take care of the endless and demanding amount of work involved with growing rice. Black men cleared acres of trees from the land. The average task for a slave was twelve hundred square feet a day. Slaves dug miles of trenches (ditches) with simple tools. Slaves also built huge banks (dams) to hold the water in the rice fields, and pulverized the ground to get it ready for planting. Women planted at least one-fourth an acre of rice each day.

Sullivan's Island was a major port of entry for enslaved Africans. Upon arrival in Charles Town, the Africans were quarantined in "pest houses" for ten to forty days out of fear that they carried contagious diseases. Two to three hundred Africans at a time would sometimes remain in isolation in the pest houses until declared healthy.

The Africans were crammed into slave ships with peasants next to African kings and princes. They were stripped of everything but their names and often their masters gave them new, more European, names. But they carried with them memories of their culture: music, folklore, social structure and religion. On the plantations of the South, the slaves multiplied and passed their African roots to their descendants in a rich and lasting tradition that we call Gullah.

Gullah is a pidgin language. According to the film series *The Adventures of English: 500 AD to 2000,* Gullah originated on the slave ships themselves. Enslaved Africans were often from different tribes and spoke different dialects. In order to communicate they were forced to create a common language. Slaves brought many African words into the English language. Those African words were later mixed with Spanish, French and English to create a complete sub-language that often sounded familiar, but to the untrained ear was absolute gibberish.

The Sea Islands of South Carolina provided a fertile environment for the survival of West African culture. These were vast plantations, isolated from the mainland, some covering thousands of acres, overseen by a small number of whites. African medicine men, erroneously called "witch doctors" by the whites, were also sold into slavery. These medicine men reinstated tribal customs; the rhythm of African drums often echoed through the Carolina nights. Through the decades, many of the white owners converted their slaves to Christianity, but the Africans mixed their tribal beliefs with Christian practices to create an unusual religious ceremony that offended and horrified many whites. But it seemed to keep peace on the plantations. There were relatively few slave rebellions on the remote Sea Islands, mainly due to the fact that as long as the plantation work continued, many slaves were left alone to live in their own tradition.

Shortly after the beginning of the Civil War, the coasts of South Carolina and Georgia fell to the U.S. Navy. Slave owners fled the area and tens of thousands of newly freed slaves flocked to federal authorities for protection and sustenance. Burdened by the care of so many, the government established the freed slaves on land confiscated from their former masters. It wasn't the "forty acres and a mule" as promised, but it was usually ten acres with no mule. For two decades after the war, Northerners came south to teach agriculture, citizenship and literacy, but by 1880 those teachers were gone and the freed slaves resumed their lives close to the soil, still isolated from the world. Even into the twenty-first century, pockets of that Gullah civilization still remain. And part of their culture includes voodoo, or as it is called in Charleston, "the Root." Gullahs still have a strong belief in the spiritual and folk customs, especially concerning the dead.

The stories of some former slaves were recorded during the Great Depression. In 1935, a quarter of the American workforce was unemployed and Congress appropriated funds for the Works Progress Administration (WPA). President Roosevelt declared that the government would provide work for the needy, and the WPA instituted the Federal Writers' Project, in which over three million field workers were instructed to interview former slaves. They were given a list of sample questions. The most interesting question was "Do you believe in spirits?" In the Lowcountry of South Carolina and Georgia, that led to hundreds of stories recorded about Gullah culture, stories that included hags, plat-eyes, boo daddies and root doctors.

A plat-eye is a creature that takes the shape of an animal: dog, mule, goat, rat, squirrel, owl, crow or cat. Plat-eyes usually stay close to graveyards and are more active during a new moon. Former slave May Ethel Pickett of Murrells Inlet, South Carolina, recounted a childhood encounter:

> *Us was going home from church. Came first a little with cat, came out of the woods, came out in the road. Us ran. And then us looked back and there was a little white dog! And us ran again. And when us looked back next there was a white mule! When us got to Grandpa's house, he said that was a plat-eye.*
>
> From WPA Narratives

"Haint" (Hants or Haants) is a generic term for any spiritual creature of the night, usually a ghost. A haint cannot hurt you unless you run away from it. Salt and sulfur will keep a ghost away. The sulfur on a match head will protect you, and sprinkling salt on your doorway will keep haints away, as well as the color blue. Former slave Frank McNeal accounts his encounter with a haint:

> *Splash! Splash! Splash! I flung open the door. There stood a woman, dressed in white, with part of her garment spread over the water's surface. All of a sudden she took off her head and threw it toward me.*

> *That same week my little boy died. He was not sick so far as anybody could say. Some folks think it's all superstition and ignorance. I believe in ghosts because I can see them.*
>
> From WPA Narratives

Sam Bailey of Edisto Island, South Carolina, accounts how he would handle ghosts:

> *I know exactly how to deal with ghosts who make a nuisance of themselves 'round my premises. I bottle them. Ain't everybody who can do that. Ghosts 'round my place kept me awake for nights on end till I learned to catch them in bottles. I spent hours preparing a charm I placed in the bottom of the bottle. I never told no one what made the charm, except one ingredient: chamber lye. The charm was so powerful ghosts couldn't help but fall in. I corked the bottle and put it under my bed. After I kept the ghosts in the bottle the entire night, them ghosts didn't bother me no more.*
>
> From WPA Narratives

According to Gullah legend haints (or haunts) can't cross water. Because of this the color blue is believed to be a powerful protection. Slaves used to live in brick cabins with no door or windows, just open holes for ventilation. They would paint the threshold of the openings blue, or hang blue cloth over the openings to keep the haints out.

Today that tradition is alive and well in Charleston. The ceilings of many of our porches are blue. Doors, shutters and, sometimes, entire houses are painted blue.

According to legend, boo-hags are similar to vampires except they do not suck your blood. A boo-hag steals energy by sucking its victim's breath, just as superstitions say a cat steals a baby's breath. This stealing of energy happens through a process known as "ridin'." A common expression heard among many in the Lowcountry is "don't let de hag ride ya'."

The presence of boo-hags may be connected to Charleston's long history of racial inequality. Much of Charleston today is built upon reused land, some of which housed colonial-era slave graveyards.

Boo-hags are most often found above these displaced burial grounds. Boo-hags have no skin and are blood red. They have a flaxen-like quality that makes them appear "raw" as well as hard to hold onto. Boo-hags also feel warm to the touch, like warm raw meat. As a result of their grotesque appearance, boo-hags often choose to disguise themselves inside of another person's skin, which they have "borrowed" for as long as the skin holds out. (The former owner of the skin is left out of luck.) Boo-hags can then wear the full skin like a suit of clothes. Thus disguised, boo-hags can freely go about their affairs and selectively choose potential candidates for ridin'.

In order to ride someone, boo-hags must first get out of their stolen skin and hide it for the return. Afterward, boo-hags will fly off to go do some ridin'. Once a potential victim has been chosen, the boo-hag will enter that person's home, normally through some type of crack or crevice like a large keyhole. Inside of the home, boo-hags will go for the bedroom where the unsuspecting victim soundly sleeps. The boo-hag will then stealthily position itself over the sleeping victims and begin sucking their breath. As the boo-hag rides, the victim will slip into a dreamlike state rendered helpless.

After the boo-hag has finished the ride, there will be little to show for the incident. The next morning a victim of boo-hag riding may feel very tired or haggard; however, they will not have been killed. The boo-hag will save you in case it ever wants to come back and ride you again. They must be back in their own skins by first light of dawn, or they are forever trapped out-of-skin.

There are court records from 1813 that indicate a trial against a witch who was accused of "slipping through the keyhole." Maulsey Stone recounts a her experience with a boo-hag:

> *Back yonder, in slavery times, when a young man came around to court, girl chillum followed along. I expects one of them girl chillum didn't like it 'cause a certain boy loved me very much. She set a hag on my track.*
>
> *The hag come to see me. I remember good when I caught sight. I was fixing to go to bed and a green light burst in before my eyes. Then I saw a black, raggedy-looking thing ascend the steps. I opened my mouth to yell, but my jaw locked. That hag rode me all that night and the next thirty-two nights. When I rose in the morning I felt like somebody had beat me with a stick.*
>
> From WPA Narratives

Penny Williams also remembered when a boo-hag entered her bedroom:

> *One night a hag tried her best to ride me. I was in bed, and she thought I was asleep. That no-skin hag came flying through the window. I felt her when she crawled up on my left leg. It felt like a jellyfish—like jelly or rubber, sticky like. The circulation stopped in that leg. Before the hag got up to my neck I got up and found a knife. I fixed that hag up good and plenty.*
>
> From WPA Narratives

A boo-daddy is the spirit of a root doctor (witch doctor) or conjure man released from his body after death for dread purposes. They torment those who do not believe in voodoo or root medicine. They can only be restrained by a charm made by another root doctor. Drolls are the spirits of young children who died a painful death. Their cries and screeches can be heard in deep swamp and marshland at night.

Have you ever woke up in the morning feeling exhausted, as if you had been exercising all night? The boo-hag been ridin' ya.

## Part Two

# Petticoats and Prostitutes—Antebellum Charleston

## Chapter Four

# Sodom and Gomorrah of the South

*"This is Charles-Town"*

*Black and white all mix'd together*
*Inconstant, strange, unhealthful weather*
*Burning heat and chilling cold*
*Dangerous both to young and old*
*Boisterous winds and heavy rains*
*Fevers and rheumatic pains*
*Agues plenty without doubt*
*Sores, boils, the prickling heat and gout*
*Water bad, past all drinking*
*Men and women without thinking*
*Every thing at a high price*
*But rum, hominy and rice*
*Many a widow not unwilling*
*Many a beau not worth a shilling*
*Many a bargain, if you strike it*
*This is Charles-town, how do you like it*

Captain Martin, 1769

## Swimming in a Swamp of Sin

In 1785, Francis Asbury established Charleston's first Methodist congregation on Cumberland Street. Bishop Asbury was horrified by the proclivity of drinking, smoking, card playing, "sexual debauchery of the most vile nature" and, of course, slavery, which was worse in his mind. In his letters, Asbury referred to Charles Town as the "Sodom and Gomorrah of the South."

Dr. Johnson B. Schoepf of New York noted: "luxury in Carolina has made the greatest advance. The people of Charleston live rapidly, not willingly letting go untasted any of the pleasures of life." Charleston embraced the cosmopolitan ideals of Paris and London with more fervor than any other American city. The ruling elite had developed into a genuine aristocracy. This was the most hedonistic society in America. It is hard to say which form of entertainment they enjoyed the most, or how they found time to take them all in.

They loved to eat, rather to dine. They ingested rich seafood dishes, pastries, tarts and rice breads. They imported wine from all over the world. They drank rum punch made from citrus fruits, which was considered exotic since they had to be imported. There was music, theatre, horse racing, cockfighting, hunting, fishing and, at the top of the list, wenching. William J. Grayson states in his autobiography that it was customary for the host of a party to lock the doors and refuse any guest to depart until he was drunk. Often, members of the legislature would get so drunk during a session they would abandon their work and march the streets singing, accompanied by drum and fiddle.

Charleston was the center for theatre in America until after the War between the States. In 1773–74, 188 performances were given in Charleston, including 11 Shakespearean plays. In the eighteenth century actors were not respectable people. England had statutes against "rogues, vagabonds, and stage-players" and those statutes were transported to America. Certainly, the Puritans in New England and the Quakers in Pennsylvania had little use for theatre. In Charleston the theatre was so accepted that the site of the first dramatic performance in the city was the court house. Charleston became a haven for traveling professional theatrical troops.

The Hallam's Company, arrived in Charles Town in the fall of 1754 and remained for three months. The American Company brought *Romeo and Juliet* and *King Lear* to Charleston. That company had been met with hostility and legal problems in New York. They arrived in Charleston in November 1763 and remained until 1766.

In 1794, a French-language playhouse opened on the west side of Church Street between St. Michael's Alley and Tradd Street. It was known as the Church Street French Theatre with a company of comedians and players, led by Paris-born ballet dancer Alexander Placide. The shows featured comedy, acrobatics, dancing and tightrope walking. Even though the theatre was successful, Placide was involved (as was most of the company) with several scandals, usually involving sexual indiscretions and gambling debts. He later opened a public pleasure ground, Vaux Hall, at the northeast corner of Broad and Friend (later Legare) Streets (present location of the Cathedral of St. John the Baptist). During the summer, patrons could attend outdoor musical events, fireworks, public baths and even ride on elephants.

For such an educated elite society, they rarely used their free time for more intellectual pursuits. Charleston had the first public library in America, but the elite published no books of any serious quantity or quality. Reading was never a favorite recreation. It had to compete with wenches and alcohol.

This lifestyle led to the ironic reality of well-bred young gentlemen involved in a social life that was deemed "low" and "lewd" by outsiders. Because of the planters' insistence on the subordination of their sons and the fact that the sons were dependent on their fathers' inheritance, an entire generation of young men spent their years after college, and before marriage, in idleness by gambling, drinking and wenching. This set the standard for the behavior of Charleston men. Many of the elite women complained that the Charleston men were "fonder of their Cards and Brandy and Segars than their Company."

It was no accident that the most famous Charlestonian of all time was a handsome, dashing, hard-drinking, womanizing (though fictional) scoundrel named Rhett Butler. He was the type of man to take a Charleston girl out in a buggy and refuse to marry her the next day. Reading *Gone With The Wind* will provide as accurate portrait of the life of an antebellum Charleston gentleman as any history book.

Men enjoyed the taverns, or "punch houses," such as Dillon's on Broad Street, the Sign of Bacchus and the Georgia Coffee House. Carl Bridenbaugh of Boston wrote: "The importation of liquors at Charles

Town staggers the imagination—1500 dozen [18,000] bottles [of ale]...1219 hogsheads [wine]...and 58 barrels of rum." This was a six-month supply for one tavern.

Taverns supplied more than drinks. There were shows, entertainments and women, all mixed in with the liquor and wine. The Planters Hotel (present location of the Dock Street Theatre) was the main hub for social occasions, entertainments, theatre and women. The upper floors of the hotel were reserved for "gentlemen and their private guests." Unlike most of America's ruling class, the men of Charleston were not reluctant to take advantage of their female slave population. Richard Hofstadter, Columbia University historian, noted: "By comparison with Charles Town's elite, the old Boston's uppercrust looked poor and flimsy...the [Charleston] hedonistic life...put the other seaboard towns in the shade."

In May 1820, in order to help revive the depressed local economy, Congress designated Charleston as one of the eight Atlantic ports where foreign-armed vessels were permitted to enter. While it did little to revive the general economy, it was a boom for the local brothels and taverns. After repeated complaints to the city council, an ordinance was passed to "forbid dance halls where women notoriously of ill fame are entertained for the purpose of dancing with persons as visit such places." But the police neglected to enforce the ordinance.

A steady stream of clients flooded the area of French Alley between Meeting and Anson Streets. In February 1835, at the northeastern corner of State and Linguard Streets (current location of Palmetto Carriage's big red barn), a fire broke out at Cornel June's boardinghouse, which was known as "a brothel of the very lowest order and degraded character." The fire burned across the city market and up Church Street. It consumed more than sixty structures including St. Philip's Church. Many non-Anglicans (Methodists in particular) considered the destruction of the church by fire to be a sign from God that He was displeased with the church.

Soon after, The Charleston Port Society for Promoting the Gospel among Seaman was organized to persuade sailors that there were "pleasures above the brothel" and to avoid "the haunts of dissipation and vice." It was a miserable failure.

John C. Calhoun hated to return home to Charleston from Washington, D.C. He was from upstate South Carolina. Calhoun served in the House of Representatives, was secretary of state during the Monroe administration, served two terms as vice president of the United States (with John

Quincy Adams and Andrew Jackson) and upon the time of his death was a U.S. senator. But Calhoun lived in Charleston because his blueblood wife refused to live elsewhere. He loathed the city, its people and their lifestyle. He said Charleston was "intemperate and full of debauchery. A disgraceful place infested with gangs of vagabonds bent on mischief."

Dr. David Ramsay agreed with Calhoun in regards to Charleston's love of alcohol. In his history of South Carolina he writes the following:

> *Drunkenness may be called an endemic vice of Carolina. The climate disposes to it, and the combined influence of religion and education, too often fail to restrain it. All these temptations to intoxication are increased by idleness. Men are so constituted as to be incapable of total stagnation. Something to stimulate the senses, employ the body or occupy the mind, is a matter of absolute necessity. He whose vacant mind cannot amuse itself with reading, reasoning, reflecting, or the reveries of imagination; whose inclination disrelishes and whose circumstances elevate him above bodily labor, has only one avenue left to save himself from the painful sensations of being without any employment for mind or body; that is, to rouse his senses by the poignancy of something that acts directly and strongly upon them.*
>
> *This may be done by tobacco, opium, and some other irritating substances, but by nothing so readily or so conveniently as by ardent spirits. The draught, which at first excited the senses, soon becomes inadequate. The quantity must therefore be increased. A pernicious habit is thus insensibly formed from having nothing to do.*
>
> *The general position being once admitted that the addition of rum, gin, brandy, or whisky, is an improvement of water, it is no easy matter to stop at the precise point of temperance. The reasoning powers are so far the dupes of sense that a little more and a little stronger is taken without hesitation. Thirst makes the first drink a plentiful one: a few supplementary draughts complete the business of intoxication, and induce an oblivion of all cares. The good natured, pleasant, accommodating youth, dies a sot before he attains to middle age.*

Not every citizen embraced drunkenness. Many agreed with Dr. Ramsay's assessment of the situation. Whiskey was cited as the principal source of crime. A grand jury in 1818 stated: "We are free in stating that three-fourths of the indictments that fill the records of our Courts of

Justice, have their origin at Tipling [*sic*] shops." Whiskey was called the "root of every sort of evil from riot to murder."

Respectable citizens fought against the tide of drunkenness. Judge John O'Neall organized "Cold Water Clubs" and once served as national chairman of the "Sons of Temperance," which was aligned with the "Daughters of Temperance." Almost every South Carolina community had a Cold Water Club. Charleston, with the largest population of the state, had two and both were ineffective. The Cold Water Clubs claimed that the situation in the city was out of control and extreme measures were needed. They lobbied lawmakers to strengthen laws regulating the sale, manufacture and use of whiskey. Some of the proposed laws included taking all property of a habitual drunkard and hanging an innkeeper caught selling whiskey to a known alcoholic!

The measures were never enacted, but the fact that the assembly seriously debated them illustrates how extreme the problem must have been.

All legal liquor dealers were to be bonded in the sum of one thousand dollars and their annual permits were charged at fifty dollars. These outrageous sums limited the number of legal dealers, and only encouraged illegal tippling houses.

To restrain drinking in barrooms and inns, a law required a retailer of spirits to sell "not less than three gallons to each customer." The theory was that no one could afford to purchase three gallons at one time, and even if they could, it could not be consumed in one sitting. The customers got around the restriction by pooling their money and having one man purchase three gallons. He would then share it with his friends.

Whiskey legislation had little effect in Charleston. Most citizens ignored the laws, as did the local police force. The police feigned ignorance by claiming all the taverns were merely serving "sweet cider." In 1830, the average American adult consumed seven gallons of alcohol per year. In Charleston, the average adult consumed twelve gallons.

The Cold Water Clubs published the following poem in an attempt to attract more support to their cause of temperance:

*Ye sons of Cold-Water, your voices now raise*
*And speak of cold water and sing to its praise*

*Its virtues are many its vices but few*
*Its life-giving powers are offered to you*

*It will do you more good than Sherry or Port*
*And save you from quarrels, from fighting and court*

*Then shun the vile tempter choose what is best*
*And drink but cold water and hate all the rest*

For such a cosmopolitan society, Charleston was a dangerous place. Ann Royall (credited as the first female American journalist) visited the city and was not impressed. She wrote:

> *Charleston, S.C., from being the garden spot of the United States, is now a receptacle for the refuse of all nations on earth; not only nations, but of jails, penitentiaries, pirate dens, &c. The inns and hotels serve as headquarters for the criminal gangs which plague the city. These public houses serve as the special accommodation of ruffians, gamblers, pick-pockets and swindlers – the landlord being the greatest swindler of the whole.*

She was right. Charleston was infested with pickpockets, forgers and counterfeiters. Often, these "sharpers" operated under the guise of teachers, physicians, lawyers or ministers. At one time a grand jury stated "there were so many fake doctors...the lives of the people were actually in danger."

One of the most infamous "sharpers" was David T. Hines. Between 1827 and 1854 he was a one-man crime wave in South Carolina until he died in jail. Hines wrote a successful book about his life, titled: *The Life, Adventures and Opinions of David Theodore Hines, of South Carolina, alias Dr. Hamilton, Col. Hamilton, Dr. Haynes, Col. Haynes, Dr. Porcher, Col. Singleton, Rev. Mr. Meman, Rev. Dr. Baker, Col. Allston, Maj. Parker, Col. Benton, Maj. Middleton, Capt. Rutledge, Col. Pinckney, Dr. Brandreth, Maj. Moore, &c, &c, &c.*

Then there was Dick Walters. Walters dyed himself brown and had a colleague sell him as a mulatto slave. After the sale, he would escape, wash off the dye, split the money with his partner and repeat the process. The problem was, after a time, his skin became permanently darkened by the treatments, which put him in the situation of being a 100 percent pure white man, commonly mistaken as half black.

The swindler most prevalent in antebellum South was, by far, the professional gambler. Gambling was a crime but the professional had little problem finding men who were willing to chance money playing dice or cards. The refugees from San Domingo had introduced all the new French games to Charleston.

Two of the best-known gaming houses were Miss Polly Rupel's on Legare Street, where "the elite of society risked their hearts and small change at cribbage," and another house on Society Street (between Meeting and Anson Streets) where the stakes were higher. Men would often lose as much as "one hundred and seventy-five dollars" in one night.

During the decades preceding the War between the States, indictment rates skyrocketed. In 1820, the indictment rate was 1 per 516; in 1840, 1 per 490; and by 1850 it was 1 per 334. Governor Pierce Butler, who believed the availability of so many weapons created violence, stated: "Only the unthinking part of the community keep weapons on their person." Using that logic, the thinkers in antebellum Charleston were in a vast minority. Pistols, knives, dirks and sword canes were as necessary a part of a man's attire as his jacket and trousers. By nightfall, most respectable citizens were home behind locked doors. The streets were too violent and dangerous.

William Faux, an English traveler, wrote in his journal that Charleston was "disgraced by thieves and cutthroats. In the street where I sleep, for two nights successively, our slumbers have been disturbed by the cries of murder!"

James Stribling, another English traveler, commented about his trip to Charleston:

> *When Herr von Hinckleday, the Prussian Minister of Police, was shot last year, the whole of Europe rang with indignant denunciation; while here, citizens murder each other and the fact is recorded as coolly as the variation of a cent a pound in the price of cotton.*

A front-page story of the March 5, 1804 Charleston *Courier* was a typical news item of the day and read: "A fracas occurred, we understand, on Monday night...between William Nelson and Joseph Williams, during which the Former was shot and the Latter severely cut...we refrain from entering into particulars."

Fourth of July and Christmas were also excuses for drunkenness and rowdy behavior. S.A. Townes described Independence Day as "a time set aside for eating bad food, listening to long speeches and dodging wild bullets. The safest place to stay is at home."

Court week was another public event that was accompanied by brawls, riots, public drunkenness and lewdness. Since the judges had to ride a large circuit, court cases were heard on a quarterly basis. People from as far as one hundred miles would arrive in town for their court hearings. Often, it was the only time country people ventured into the city. Court week became an excuse for drinking and celebration. Even members of the jury got into the spirit. An 1807 court record indicates that "Juror John Nelson was discovered to be too drunk to sit, and his relief, Henry Ford, had apparently slipped out of court." In ten days of that court session, twenty-one jurors were deemed too incapacitated to serve, or were in no condition to appear. Judging by other court records, that was not an unusual circumstance.

Judge John Faucheraud Grimke once presided in a trial where the defendant entered a plea of guilty. The jury put their heads together and announced a verdict of "not guilty." The judge was aghast. He asked, "How could you return such a verdict, after his confession?" The jury foreman replied, "Why, he's always been such a liar we're not going to believe him now."

Benjamin Perry, lawyer and future governor, once successfully defended a swindler. After being acquitted, the criminal paid the lawyer with fake money, and left town.

Judge Elihu Hall Bay, known as the stuttering judge, was deaf and crotchety in his old age. He once sentenced two culprits for biting. He ordered the two put in the same cell and remarked, "you may bite one another as much as you please."

Murder trials were the high points of court week. Most murders were not for financial gain. It was due to an insult, real or imagined, or the result of an argument mixed with alcohol. Most murders were not committed with firearms but with knives, rocks, clubs and axes. Most feared of all, however, was poison. The fear stemmed from the idea that Negro slaves were skilled in its use.

During this period, misdemeanors included the crimes of public swearing, Sabbath-breaking and several sex offenses (other than rape). Bastardy accounted for 3 percent of criminal indictments. Until 1847, the bastardy law in South Carolina forced the convicted father to pay about twenty-five dollars a year toward the upkeep of the child. Should the father not be able to pay, he was to be sold to the highest bidder at public auction as an indentured servant, and his wages would go to the child.

For buggery (sodomy) the penalty was death, but convictions were hard to obtain. There was at least one buggery scandal in Charleston, concerning a "well-known lawyer" in 1795.

Bigamy was more common, but usually treated as simple adultery. John Sloan was accused of "creeping to bed with Elizabeth Alexander in the night time in a disorderly manner." Another court document reads: "Edward Ramsey and Nancy Grubs, Thomas Wosdon & Polly Grubs, and Bolan Grubs and a free Negro woman are living in a state of lewdness and fornication to the great annoyance of the good people of the upper part of the District."

One document declared, "Open adultery has of late become so common and notorious as to render social order insecure...and load our Country with indigent orphans and prostitutes." In 1844, George W. Williams introduced a bill in the House of Representatives making adultery and co-habitation a serious offence. It failed to pass.

Justice was quick and often brutal. In 1813, there were 165 crimes that carried the death penalty. In 1825, that number was down to 51. In 1838, it was down to 32, and by 1859 the number had dropped to 22. South Carolina consistently led all states in offenses punishable by hanging.

Hanging was a public spectacle and was advertised weeks before the event. People came from miles on foot, horseback and by wagon. They brought picnic baskets, or purchased "lunch boxes" sold by local inns and taverns. The gallows were constructed in a large open place to give the public a good view of the "swinging-off." Often, wooden "spectator benches" (bleachers) would be erected. It was a festive and colorful occasion. There were "dandies with extravagantly-cut pantaloons"; "coon-skinned capped wagoners"; soldiers from the garrison at Fort Johnson; Dutch, French and Spanish seamen; "country cousins who had come to town"; "free Negroes with their plump mulatto wives"; and both slaves and white apprentice boys all gathered about the gibbet. Little masters and little misses broke from their nurses. Here and there were even fashionably clad women; the keepers of grog shops and sailors' boardinghouses in Bedon's Alley were there. The girls from the houses were there, on their best behavior.

There was a moment of silence as the victim was prepared, and usually a cheer after the criminal was "launched into eternity." Branding was done in the courtyard by the sheriff. One of three letters *T*, *M* or *F* were branded on the cheek, thumb or forehead. *M* was for manslaughter; *T* was for a thief; and *F* was for a bigamist, adulterer or fornicator. Brandings, like hangings, were also well attended.

If one was convicted of petty larceny, or manslaughter, the judge often sentenced the criminal to the pillory. Standing in the pillory was a common practice. The pillory was a solid wood frame with holes through which the offender's head and arms were placed and held fast and was usually erected in the courtyard near the whipping post. The person standing in the pillory was accosted by the passing citizens, derided, insulted and often pelted by rotten vegetables, eggs and human waste. A person sentenced to the pillory stood for periods from half an hour to several hours.

Whipping was also a common punishment. The judge would assign a specific number of lashes. Whipping posts were two poles connected by a cross beam to which the criminal's arms would be secured. Charleston had the most elaborate whipping post in South Carolina. It was commonly called the "Crane of Pain." The victim would stand between the two posts, ankles lashed securely, then two ropes that dangled from the top crossbeam through a pulley system would be secured around the victim's wrists. The ropes would be pulled higher and higher until the victim was completely stretched taunt—exposing his bare back and chest. The sheriff would administer the lashes, using the Biblical standard, "forty lashes, save one," while someone else would call out the number of each lash.

## DAVID AND MARTHA RAMSAY—INTERTWINED LIVES AND DEATHS

Martha was a cherished child. At the time of her birth her father, Henry Laurens, was one of the richest men in the colonies. One of the largest slave importers in America, Laurens typified the elite of Charles Town society. Educated, rich and infused with a public spirit, Laurens felt that, due to their position, he and his family had an obligation to serve the public good. All the Laurens children absorbed their father's public service spirit, and it became part of their duty. As Laurens wrote in his papers, "private interest must not be set in competition with public good."

Martha became cherished at age seven months, when she contracted smallpox and was pronounced dead by Dr. John Moultrie, Martha's godfather. Her small body was immediately wrapped in a shroud and laid out by an open window in anticipation of a quick burial. That was a common occurrence during this time, as an outbreak of any infectious disease sent the population into panic. Dr. Moultrie left to arrange grave preparations in the Circular Church cemetery. Six hours later Dr. Moultrie returned to accompany the body to the hastily prepared gravesite. Laurens asked to see his daughter once more. Dr. Moultrie opened the shroud and both men were stunned to see her tiny nostrils flaring. He concluded the fresh air coming through the window had revived her. Shortly after that incident, her father wrote a codicil in his will ordering his body to be cremated after a three-day waiting period to make sure he could not be buried alive. From that day, Martha became the apple of her father's eye.

Laurens demanded that all his children be educated, not just the males. Martha could read at an early age and was taught math and science at a high level, unusual for a woman of that time. Martha liked to show off an unusual talent: the ability to read any book upside down. Being a merchant, Laurens insisted his children work on their penmanship. He praised Martha as having "a perfect hand." For years she was the official bookkeeper for her father.

Martha lived through calamitous times. At midnight on October 23, 1765, the Laurens house was stormed by a group of men who called themselves "Sons of Liberty." Henry Laurens had taken the unpopular public position of supporting the Stamp Act of 1765. The invaders searched the house looking for the offending stamps that had arrived in the city through Laurens's import house that day. Her father, who served in the Continental Congress, gradually became in favor of independence due in part to his friendship with a young Frenchman named Marie Joseph Paul Yves Roche Gilbert du Motier, or the Marquis de Lafayette.

When Martha was eleven years old she suffered the deaths of her older sister, Nellie, and her mother. She became the woman of the Laurens household. In 1775, when Martha was sixteen, Henry Laurens sent her and younger sister Polly to England to live with her brother, Henry Jr., for safety. Laurens could see that soon America would be plunged into full-scale war and, due to his duties as president of the Continental Congress he wanted his daughters out of harm's way. Laurens's brother James and his wife escorted them. It was at this time in her life that Martha began the keeping of a daily journal that forms the basis of much of what we know about her life.

During the voyage to England, Martha told her uncle James that "Jemmy died last night." Jemmy was Martha's ten-year-old brother, attending school in London. She urged her uncle to write down the time and date of their conversation. When they arrived in England, Henry Jr. informed the family that Jemmy had died due to an accidental fall that resulted in a concussion.

In 1778, Henry Laurens was on a diplomatic mission to Europe. He was captured on the open seas by the British and imprisoned in the Tower of London, the first American to be held there. Martha's oldest brother, John, was serving on the staff of George Washington and their family friend Lafayette was helping the Americans against the British. Martha and Polly moved to France for safety.

Her father fared badly in the tower. Conditions were appalling. Vindictive guards often withheld food and clothing. Martha took charge of the family. She lobbied the American diplomats in Europe, John Adams and Benjamin Franklin, to help her father. When those men were ineffectual, she lobbied to the British directly. She was told by the British, "we will keep Mr. Laurens to hang as a traitor after the war is won in our favor."

Laurens was freed from the tower on January 1, 1782, and was escorted to Paris by John Jay. Martha and Polly met their father and helped nurse him back to health. During this period she woke her father in the middle of the night, August 28, 1782, and told him "John is dead." Like she had done with her uncle, she urged her father to write down the time and date of her pronouncement. One month later, news of John's death arrived in a letter.

Even in his weakened condition, Laurens fulfilled his duties to his new country. On November 30, 1782, Laurens, along with John Jay, Benjamin Franklin and John Adams, became one of the signatories of the Treaty of Paris, formally ending the American Revolution. Martha was twenty-one years old and sitting at her father's side during the entire negotiation, journal in her lap, keeping the official record of the event for the American government.

Four years later, Martha arrived back in Charleston with her father and almost immediately met Dr. David Ramsay. Ramsay had been imprisoned in St. Augustine during the Revolution. He had spent his time composing a history of the Revolution, almost completely from memory. The young doctor and budding historian requested access to Henry Lauren's papers for his research. He and Martha spent many hours going through letters and journals and two years later, she became Mrs. David Ramsay. She called her marriage a "joint pilgrimage here on earth."

In addition to affection and intelligence, the couple had an odd, yet powerful connection. Martha had almost died of smallpox, and inadvertently almost been buried alive, and Ramsay had lost the sight of one eye due to the disease. Ramsay became the first doctor in America to import and use a French smallpox vaccine. The first patient was their oldest child, David Ramsay Jr.

Henry Laurens died not long after his daughter's marriage and Martha supervised his cremation. As it was laid out in his will, he was buried after the three-day waiting period.

Martha gave birth to ten children, eight who survived her. Their life in Charleston was modest, but productive. Dr. Ramsay published his history, now considered the first published history of the American Revolution and it is still in print and quoted earlier in this chapter. The affection Martha had for her father is revealed in the names of her girls: Eleanor Henry Laurens Ramsay, Martha Henry Laurens Ramsay, Frances Henry Laurens Ramsay and Catherine Henry Laurens Ramsay.

In her last years Martha became involved with Methodism. She and her husband both read John Wesley's *Thoughts on Slavery* that stated all "Christians be able to exercise their own free will." In 1792, Dr. Ramsay stated publicly in the legislature, "We firmly believe that the further importation of slave is contrary to the true interests of Carolina." The daughter of one of the largest slave traders in America was now opposed to the very commodity that created her family's massive wealth. It made the Ramsays at odds with 99 percent of their neighbors.

Martha was kept busy educating her children and running the household of a prominent man. Ramsay was a member of the legislature and a noted writer and lecturer who traveled often. But she still found time to dabble in sketching. In 1803, she gave a sketch of a church to Robert Mills, a young local architect who had studied with Thomas Jefferson. Mills liked the sketch so much that he actually designed a structure from the picture—the 1802 structure that was called the Circular Church. Mills later built the Washington Monument and U.S. Treasury building.

Martha died on June 10, 1811. Her papers included all directions for her burial: the coffin, the clothing for her body and the funeral service itself. During the last moments of her life she gathered her entire family around her and asked each if they were "willing to give me up."

Two weeks after her death, Dr. Ramsay made the decision to edit and publish his wife's diary. Two years later, it was published as the *Memoirs of Martha Laurens Ramsay*, a detailed look into the mind and times of an extraordinary woman.

Martha's story does not end with her death. After the publication of her memoirs, Dr. Ramsay was appointed by the court to pass judgment on the mental condition of William Linnen. Linnen was a tailor making continual threats against lawyers and judges who had ruled against him in several court cases. Ramsay ruled the man insane, but two other physicians ruled Linnen mentally competent. On May 8, 1813, as Ramsay was walking home to lunch, standing in the shadow of St. Michael's Church, the deranged tailor shot Ramsay three times in the back. He was carried to his house where he died three days later.

On his deathbed, with the children gathered around him Ramsay said: "I have talked with your mother and she urges me to forgive the man due to his illness. She also insists I forgive my fellow physicians for their misdiagnosis. If that is the price I pay to rejoin her, I pay it gladly."

He died less than one hour later.

## A MESSAGE TO HELL—LOVELY LAVINIA

> *Execution—The awful sentence of the law is this day to be carried into effect upon John Fisher and Lavinia, his wife, who were sentenced to death, at the late sitting of the Constitutional Court, for the crime of highway robbery. We understand that they are to meet their fate just without the lines, on the Meeting-Street Road, between the hours of 12 and 4 o'clock.*
>
> Friday, February 18, 1820, Charleston Courier

On a cold Thursday afternoon, February 18, 1819, a group of thirty men rode north out of Charleston. They were gathered in what was termed "Lynch's Law," a group of citizens banded together to protect their interests. They had no legal authority, only the moral authority of their community. The wagon trade was being disrupted.

The wagon trade was vital to Charleston's economy. Covered wagons traveled from upstate South Carolina and western North Carolina to the port city, carrying all manner of goods: cotton, animal skins, fruits, vegetable and grains. The wagon traders were a rough and brawling lot, but during the past months the wagon trade had been plagued by attacks from a criminal gang. The rumor placed the members of the gang at over forty men and they were using local inns as their headquarters. Not only had the wagons themselves been looted, but the wagon traders had been robbed while staying overnight at inns outside the city, or lured into crooked gambling games. All in all, life was dangerous on the highway approaching Charleston, and many of the wagon trade were bypassing the city, heading to Savannah to conduct business.

But most disturbing of all was that wagon traders and other travelers had disappeared. The Lynch's Law mob was determined to discover the truth.

They rode north from the city, along what today is Rivers Avenue (Highway 52) until they reached Five Mile Road, and the Five Mile House. It was rumored to be the one of the places that harbored the criminals. The owner later admitted that the highwaymen had moved in without a "by your leave" and proceeded to take over his business. He was happy for the opportunity to be rid of the intruders; however, he probably didn't expect to have his business burned to the ground.

The Charleston men surrounded the house and sent a group inside. They gave the occupants of the Five Mile House fifteen minutes to vacate, but the criminals began to fire weapons through the windows. The Lynch's Law mob promptly set fire to the house and the outbuildings. Soon, the criminals were fleeing the structures and disappeared into the woods.

The mob did not pursue them but proceeded down the road to the Six Mile House, which was located at the current intersection of Dorchester Road and Rivers Avenue. The Six Mile House was a traditional Charleston house, three stories with a piazza along the side. There the Charleston mob repeated their actions by surrounding the house and sending several men inside. This time, the criminals peacefully packed up and vacated.

The mob left behind a young man, David Ross, in charge of the Six Mile House. The men returned to Charleston, confident they had solved the problem.

However, the next morning, two men entered the Six Mile House. Ross recognized both. One was John Fisher, a criminal and lowlife, and the other was William Heyward, a man well known to the local authorities. Heyward and Fisher attacked Ross, knocking him to the ground and telling Ross he must leave. Ross asked if he could go to his room and gather his things. Heyward pulled out a pistol. "You lay your hands on any thing, I'll kill you," he said, "Now, git!"

Ross stood and discovered the door was blocked. Two other men, and a woman, stood behind him. He recognized the woman—Lavinia Fisher. Lavinia was the type of woman most men would remember. Ross had seen her in Charleston recently and asked who she was. She was the wife of the lowlife John Fisher. Ross discovered he envied the lowlife. How could such a man attract and keep such a woman?

Lavinia was young and graceful in her walk and manner. Even though her country clothing paled in comparison with some of the finery of Charleston ladies, she was as vivacious and appealing as any woman Ross had seen on a Charleston street. Even that day, in a cold dim morning, she looked as radiant as an angel.

It was to that angel that Ross turned, as he stood surrounded by rough men. She approached him and before he could speak, she grabbed him by the throat and choked him. With her free arm she boxed him several times and thrust his head through a windowpane, slicing his face and neck. Ross managed to wrench free and when he turned she spat in his face and yelled, "You son of a bitch!" Then she spat in his face again. "You heard him. Git!"

Ross ran through the front door, half blinded with blood. He slipped and skidded across the frozen dirt. He heard two bullets whistle past as he ran. He wiped his eyes clear and turned. Heyward stood on the piazza, taking potshots, with Lavinia and John laughing.

According to an affidavit by John Peoples, on file at the county court house, this is what happened next. Later that morning, about eleven o'clock, less than two hours after Ross had made his escape, Peoples arrived at the Six Mile House. He had finished his business in Charleston and had stopped to water his horses on his way back to Georgia. A young boy was filling a bucket so Peoples waited. A drunken man stumbled out of the house and told the boy, "Give me that bucket." The boy refused, saying he needed it for his water. The man lunged at the boy and Peoples, in an attempt to protect the boy, flicked his whip at the man.

The man flew into a rage, screaming and shouting. Almost immediately nine or ten persons, including a woman, poured out of the house, armed with clubs, pistols and knives and attacked Peoples. In his affidavit Peoples claimed "most active" in the brawl was the woman. She attacked Peoples with a stick, cutting his face. But as suddenly as the attack commenced, it stopped. Everyone stomped back inside.

Peoples decided not to water his horses. He put the whip to the animals but as he was pulling away two men ran out of the house. They pulled pistols and hopped onto the wagon. They robbed him of forty dollars. Peoples was going to ignore the attack and continue home, but with the theft of his money he reported both the attack and robbery to the authorities. When he arrived at the sheriff's office that afternoon, Ross was already there, his face bandaged, and giving the official statement of his incident.

The story of Peoples's assault created a furor. By all reason, the situation at the Six Mile House had to be addressed by the authorities.

The next afternoon sheriff's deputy Nathaniel Green Cleary and a "party of gentlemen" set out for the Six Mile House. They arrived at dusk, and Cleary deployed his men around the house. Inside, the gang discussed what to do. They were armed with ten muskets with fixed bayonets and a keg of powder, but the group outside was too large and determined. An attempt to fight their way out would be certain death.

Say what you will about the character of John Fisher—above all else, he loved Lavinia. He surrendered, rather than expose her to danger. Five people were arrested and the Six Mile House was burned to the ground. The prisoners were taken to the city jail. Deputy Cleary ordered them brought down into the damp, cold basement one at a time to be arraigned before a crowd of twenty citizens. Peoples and Ross were in the crowd and they both identified Heyward and John Fisher.

Then Lavinia was ushered in. With her arms bound behind her back, she appeared before the crowd, scared and shivering. Her clothes, never resplendent, were dirty and disheveled, her face streaked with mud. Yet, she was still a vision. She was a beauty, a beauty in a beast of a building. She was arraigned and jailed on suspicion of highway robbery—a swinging offense.

The old Charleston jail still stands on Magazine Street and its exterior has changed little since Lavinia was imprisoned behind its harsh bars. Its windows were described as "iron glass" metal bars, which allowed mosquitoes and rodents free rein of the facility. In the winter it was damp and cold; during the summer it sweltered with humidity and the dank aroma of human waste and sweat permeated every inch. Each cell had an iron ring in the floor to secure dangerous prisoners. The floors and inner walls were thick oak. However, the warden of the jail had never had a husband and wife imprisoned together. In deference to Lavinia, she and John were kept together in a six- by eight-foot cell on the third floor, which was usually reserved as debtor's prison. It was the less secure section of the building.

The neighborhood that surrounded the jail had once served as a potter's field, where hundreds of corpses of those too poor to pay for burial had been dumped for decades. Next door was the "Sugar House," the prison and the work house for Negroes.

While John and Lavinia waited for trial, the coroner Henry Stevens was at work. A grave that contained two skeletons was discovered less than two hundred feet from the Six Mile House. One was of a white man, and the second was of a Negro girl. Peter Neilsen, who was living in Charleston at the time and wrote a book of the Fisher affair ten years later, claimed that the Six Mile Gang "had for years carried on a complete trade of murdering and robbing. On the digging around this den of iniquity, a great number of skeletons were found, no doubt the remains of unfortunate travelers."

However, according to news accounts of the day, only two bodies were found on the premises. Another account claimed that only four months after the Six Mile House was burned, some people were digging through the rubble and discovered the grisly contents of several bodies buried in shallow graves in the cellar. The actual truth may never be known.

On May 27, 1819, John and Lavinia were brought to trial at the courthouse. During the trial John sat stone-faced, while his wife wept and shuddered in fear. It didn't take long for the jury to return a verdict—guilty of highway robbery. Their lawyer petitioned the court for a new trial before the Constitutional Court (the forerunner of the Court of Appeals) and it was granted. The Fishers had an eight-month reprieve. They would still be kept in the jail, but they would be together and alive.

They were not idle during those eight months. John and Lavinia dreamed of escape, and made plans for it. On the night of Monday, September 13, John and Rene Roberts, another man on the third floor, made a rope of the blankets that served as their mattresses. Roberts squeezed through the bars and shimmied down the side of the building. John followed with Lavinia waiting, peering through the bars as her husband lowered himself. Twenty feet from the ground, the line broke. John landed safely, but the two men stood helplessly on the ground, staring up at the small face peering down at them in the moonlight, and the broken rope at their feet.

John had a plan for the three of them to board a schooner in the harbor, bound for Cuba. Without his wife, he refused to leave town. Two days later the men were still in town, working out a plan to free Lavinia.

That Tuesday evening, after eleven o'clock, William Bull was still working in his grocery store on South Bay Street (currently South

Battery). It was a clear night, with a bright moon. He noticed two men come ashore in a small canoe. One walked off into the dark street, but the other man entered the store and bought a few items. Bull watched the man return to the water and slip beneath an overturned boat on the wharf. Bull contacted the city guard.

Ten minutes later Roberts and John Fisher were dragged from beneath the boat, and once the guard realized who they were, the men were marched back to jail. John was reunited with Lavinia. The two men were in possession of gold coins and several watches. Most likely, the two men had been on a robbery spree, trying to gather enough money to bribe a turnkey in the jail into releasing Lavinia.

No matter, John and Lavinia were now heavily guarded. In January 1820, the Constitutional Court convened. The judge rejected their motion for a new trial and set their execution date as February 4. Only the governor could save them now, and he did give them a respite of ten days. According to the *Courier*, the Fishers asked for "an opportunity for repentance...and for time to meet their God."

Most Christians approved of the decision, but many of the citizens were cynical. February 4 was during the middle of race week, the most important social event of the year. There were so many festivities; no one really wanted to be distracted with a hanging.

Every day during their respite the pastor of the First Baptist Church, Reverend Richard Furman, visited them. Furman found John Fisher to be eager and earnest in his conversations, and converted before the time of death. Lavinia was another matter. Each time Furman entered the cellblock she would leap to the bars, eyes wide and ask, "the pardon?" When she was told, "not today," she would break into curses, call the reverend a "bastard" and "son of a bitch" and spit at his feet. She would turn and sit with her back to the minister for the rest of his visit. Fourteen days she waited. Fourteen times she was disappointed.

February 18, 1820, dawned sunny, not too cold. The gallows had been built on the Meeting Street Road (Meeting Street) past Boundary Street (present-day Calhoun Street) at about the present intersection of Line Street. A crowd of several hundred had gathered in the field in the morning, eating and drinking, entertaining themselves with gossip and nervous expectation. Even the working girls from the bordellos close to the jail were there, and on good behavior.

At 12:45 p.m. the Fishers were led from the jail. Reverend Furman had spent a few moments with them in the building. When he asked Lavinia to pray, she screamed, shrieked and cursed. John prayed. They were fitted with loose white robes over their clothes, the traditional garb for the condemned. At the top of the stairs, Lavinia met the hangman.

A more wretched human creature would be hard to imagine. The hangman lived to drink, forget and execute. His emaciated body could barely cast a shadow at noon. His face, a gaunt skeletal mask of humanity, revealed nothing. He stared at the world through cold gray eyes, bloodshot from his latest bout with the bottle. He had been locked up in the jail for two days to keep him sober. Once his charges were deceased, he would be free once again to roam the streets in his drunken stupor, until the next execution day.

When Lavinia caught sight of the hangman, she shrieked again and had to be restrained by several turnkeys. The hangman shackled and chained the Fishers and led them down the stairs to a waiting coach on Magazine Street. John and Lavinia descended arm in arm. They climbed into the coach, side by side. Seated across them was the Reverend Furman, Bible in his hand, and the hangman, stone-faced with hands fidgeting together.

A company of constables escorted the coach on horseback. Slowly, the procession rolled toward their justice. Along the route, the streets were lined with the curious, some staring in silence, others jeering and cheering. Lavinia sobbed against her husband. John sat in stoic silence. Reverend Furman held his Bible. The hangman stared into some vacant vision.

Upon arrival at the gallows, they were escorted to the top separately. John stumbled on the first step, but quickly regained himself and for a moment stood silently on the scaffold, gazing at the enormous crowd gathered to witness his demise.

Lavinia refused to go. She screamed, she shrieked, she struggled. It took four constables to hold her and drag her to the stand. The crowd responded with jeers and shouts. Lavinia screamed and stamped her feet in rage, spewing forth vulgarities that some of the men had never uttered. "Damn the governor who will kill a woman!" she shouted.

Once she had been quieted, John was given the opportunity to address the crowd. In a calm voice he begged for forgiveness to any in the crowd he had injured. Lavinia was offered her chance for a statement. Resigned to her fate, she said, in a quiet voice, "If you have a message for hell, give it to me—I'll carry it."

With that, the hangman secured his ropes, pulled down the caps over their faces and he awaited the sheriff's signal. When the sheriff dropped his arm, the hangman dropped his charges. Lavinia died without a struggle. John danced for several minutes until he was still. It was just after two o'clock in the afternoon. Their bodies were carried and buried in a potter's field, the location of which has traditionally been known as the former marching grounds for the cadets at Porter Military Academy.

By nightfall, the hangman had returned to his natural state; he was drunk.

The morning of Monday, February 19, 1820, the following story appeared in the Charleston *Courier*:

> *The execution of John and Lavinia Fisher, for Highway Robbery, took place yesterday, in the suburbs of the city, agreeably to the sentences. They were taken from the jail about a quarter before 1 o'clock, in a carriage, in which, besides the prisoners was the Rev. Dr. Furman and an officer of the police. They were guarded by the Sheriff of the District, with his assistants, and a small detachment of cavalry.*
>
> *Arrived at the fatal spot, some time was spent in conversation and prayer. Fisher protested his innocence of the crime for which he was to die at last, but admitted that he had lived a wicked and abandoned life. He met his fate with great firmness; and expressed his obligations to the new Sheriff for his kindness and humanity. His wife did not display so much of fortitude or resignation – She appeared to be impressed with a belief, to the last moment, that she would be pardoned. A little past 2 o'clock the husband and wife embraced each other on the platform, for the last time in this world, when the fatal signal was given – the drop fell – and they were launched into eternity. She died without a struggle or a groan; but it was some minutes before he expired and ceased to struggle. After hanging the usual time, their bodies were taken down and conveyed to Potter's Field, where they were interred.*
>
> *The concourse that attended the execution was immense. May the awful example strike deep into their hearts; and may it have the effect intended, by deterring others from pursuing those vicious paths which end in infamy and death.*

*Author's Note: I include this, one of Charleston's most famous legends, for one reason—because most people only know the legend. There are as many versions of this story as there are tour guides. Every tour guide has a different version and, as the years pass, the versions become more lurid and spectacular.*

*When I tell my customers the "real" version, they often try to correct me by saying, "No, no, she was hanged in her wedding dress." No, sorry, she wasn't. And the number of bodies discovered was a grand total of two, not fifteen. Like all legends, Lavinia Fisher's story is founded on hard fact, blown out of proportion by time and human nature. This is my attempt to separate fact from legend.*

# Chapter Five

# The Denmark Vesey Conspiracy

Elias Horry (Charleston gentleman):
*"What were your intentions?"*
John Horry (slave):
*"To kill you, rip open your belly, and throw your guts in your face."*

In 1976 the city of Charleston commissioned a portrait of Denmark Vesey to be placed in the new municipal auditorium. The problem was 154 years after his execution no one knew what Vesey had looked like. There were no previous portraits, drawings or any physical descriptions of the man. The artist solved that problem by painting Vesey with his back to the picture, addressing a group of followers who are facing forward.

But there were other problems. In response to the portrait being commissioned, a white citizen wrote in a letter to editor of the *News and Courier*, "We should also hang portraits of Hitler, Attila the Hun and Herod the murderer of babies." The newspaper had commented on the portrait by writing, "If black leaders in Charleston had searched for a thousand years they could not have found a local black whose portrait would have been more offensive to many white people."

What did Denmark Vesey do to warrant such passions after 154 years? He planned, organized and nearly executed what would have been the largest, most violent slave rebellion in the American colonies. If not for a series of chance opportunities, more than a thousand whites would have been slaughtered in 1822.

## Charleston Conditions

"Is it possible that any of my slaves could go to heaven, and must I see them there?" This was the attitude of a female parishioner in Charles Town in 1706, as recorded by the Reverend Doctor Francis Le Jau. The reverend later commented that he could not prevail upon the people to "make a difference between Slaves and free Indians, and Beasts."

By 1800 Charleston possessed the most concentrated population of Africans in the United States. It was the fourth largest city in America, exceeded only by New York, Boston and Philadelphia. According to the 1790 census Charleston was home to 15,402 whites and 51,585 blacks. Less than 10 percent of the white population controlled most of the wealth and political power. Charleston had a larger African population than New York, Boston and Philadelphia combined, and white fears demanded that the city be run as a quasi police state. Slaves were forbidden to appear in daylight wearing fine clothes, smoking, playing an instrument or carrying a walking stick. Every evening at dusk a drum was beaten for several minutes at the guard house (current site of the U.S. Post Office at 83 Broad Street). The drum was the signal for all blacks within the city limits to disappear from the public streets until sunrise. Any black caught on the streets at night without a written pass from his master would be sent to the work house until the following morning. During the night he would be whipped and kept in a small cramped cell, chained to the wall until his master came to retrieve him by paying a small fine.

As early as 1739 there was a work house at 15 Magazine Street. The first work house was a former sugar warehouse, which led to an odd euphemism; a white master would threaten his slave that he would be sent "for a little sugar" if his bad behavior continued. "Getting sugar" meant flogging and walking the treadmill. Slaves walked on the treadmill in shifts, providing power for grinding corn. If an exhausted slave tripped and fell on the ever-moving treadmill, he often would lose a foot or leg between the rollers. Overseers used rawhide whips to maintain order. Rawhide was preferred because it flayed the skin and bruised the muscle tissue beneath. In 1769 two slaves, Dolly and Liverpoole, were burned to death on the work house green for poisoning a white infant in their care.

On August 20, 1791, there was a slave rebellion in the French colony of St. Domingue. During the next two months 180 sugar plantations and 900 coffee and cotton settlements were burned as slaves revolted, dragging their white masters from their homes and slaughtering them like livestock. Refugees poured into American cities; 500 arrived in Charleston in 1792, bringing with them their personal house slaves. A letter in a Charleston newspaper complained that the slaves from the French colony would spread the word of the successful revolt to other slaves, putting an idea in their heads. The letter complained about the city's lack of military preparation, but if anyone took the advice to heart, nothing was done.

## A Boy Named Telemaque

Slave trader Captain Joseph Vesey arrived in Haiti in 1781 with a cargo of 390 slaves from the Danish Virgin Islands. One of the slaves on board was an intelligent and handsome fourteen-year-old boy called Telemaque. The crew treated the boy like a pet, allowing him out of the hell of the cargo hold to roam above decks and perform chores for the crew; however, once in Haiti, Telemaque was sold and began to chop sugarcane for twelve hours a day. Three months later, Captain Vesey returned to the island and was accosted by an angry plantation owner who complained that Telemaque was unfit for work. Evidently, the boy suffered epileptic fits and the owner demanded a refund. Vesey returned the money and collected the boy, whom he renamed Denmark Vesey, and for the next two years the boy served as the captain's personal assistant on the slave ship.

Denmark was an unusual slave. He had a position of authority above decks on Vesey's ship. Denmark spoke several languages including Dutch, French and English fluently, as well as some Gullah and Creole, and he was invaluable to his master during his slave-buying trips up and down the west coast of Africa. However favored Denmark was, life on a slave ship was brutal, even for the crew and captain. During the eighteenth century, sailors claimed that on a calm sea they could smell a slave ship five miles away. Many white sailors refused to ship out on a vessel that had been used as a slaver, for reasons of hygiene and superstition. Some slave captains would dispose of any cargo that was not healthy enough to survive the voyage, dumping weak and diseased living Africans into the Atlantic Ocean. Charleston newspapers complained about the litter of black corpses along the local beaches. What other horrors and brutality the teenaged Denmark witnessed during his years working and living on a slave-trading ship can only be imagined. It could not have heightened his opinion of whites or of slavery.

By 1790, Captain Vesey had sold his ships, purchased property in Charleston and set up business as a moderately successful merchant at 27¼ Bay Street. He was listed in the 1790 census as head of a household, and owned eight slaves, including Denmark. For the next seventeen years Denmark was a slave in the city, often being hired out by his master to construct ships and buildings. Vesey also let Denmark keep some of the money earned, or the clever slave managed to withhold some of the sums. In 1793 Joseph Vesey was one of the men contracted to oversee the construction of the new "City Market" and it is almost certain that his skilled slave Denmark would be involved in the market construction. The Market sits on what used to be Daniel's Creek. The Pinckney family had owned the area and in 1788 the land was conveyed to the city by Charles Cotesworth Pinckney, who was a Revolutionary War general and signer of the U.S. Constitution. The purpose of the gift was "to lay out a street from the channel of the Cooper River to Meeting Street 100 feet broad, and in said street to establish a public market or markets for the purpose of vending all sorts of butcher meats, poultry, game, fish vegetables and provisions." The Market quickly became the almost exclusive domain of blacks. It was such a nasty place, filled with half-rotted meats, fish and vegetables, that few whites ventured into the area. They preferred to allow the blacks free reign in the Market, operating the food distribution of the city almost carte blanche. Large groups of blacks congregating in the pungent, muddy streets along the Market became commonplace. For that reason, thirty years later, Denmark would choose the Market as a gathering place for one of his armed companies on the night of the 1822 rebellion.

In early December 1799, Denmark used some of his "hired out" funds to purchase a ticket in the East Bay Street lottery. He bet on the numbers 1, 8, 8 and 4. By the middle of January 1800, Denmark was informed that he held the winning ticket number and he received fifteen hundred dollars. With six hundred dollars he was able to purchase his freedom from his master and then began a successful career as a free black artisan, a highly skilled carpenter. With the remaining nine hundred dollars he was able to rent and later purchase a house at 20 Bull Street, three blocks from the private residences of both the governor of South Carolina and the mayor of Charleston. He began to worship at the African Methodist Episcopalian (AME) Church, an exclusively black congregation. He also took on several women as his wives, one living with him and others who were slaves owned by other whites. He was reported to have as many of seven wives at one time in the Charleston area.

Denmark became one of about fourteen hundred free blacks living within the city, the majority of whom were mulattoes, usually the illegitimate offspring of white masters and female slaves who had been given their freedom. Denmark cut his ties with the free mulatto society who often tried to emulate white behavior by copying their lifestyle and owning slaves. Indeed, one of Denmark's neighbors, a free mulatto named Robert Smyth, owned six slaves. Since pre-Revolutionary days there had been a Charleston tradition in which Negro and mulatto women would invite white gentlemen to a ball. Most of the mulattoes felt a closer kinship with the whites than with blacks. They even avoided the exclusively black AME church and worshiped at the traditional Anglican churches of St. Philip's and St. Michael's.

Denmark became a leader of the AME church in Charleston. At a time when most blacks (free or slave) could not read or write, Denmark was well read and fluent in several languages. During his time as a church leader he began to teach passages from the Bible, which he claimed showed a moral imperative for freedom, much as the leaders of the 1960s civil rights movement did one hundred and forty years later. Denmark conducted Bible lessons at church, in his home and in slaves' quarters throughout the Charleston area. When someone objected to Denmark's vision of a violent revolution he would state, "The Lord has commanded it." The passages that he seemed to emphasize the most were:

> Colossians 4:1: *Masters, give unto your servant that which is just and equal; knowing that ye also have a Master in heaven.*
> Exodus 2: 23–24: *and the children of Israel sighed by reason of the bondage, and they cried, and their cry came up onto the God by reason of the bondage.*

Joshua 6:21: *And they utterly destroyed all that were in the city, both man and woman, both young and old.*
Zechariah 14:1–2: *Behold, the day of the Lord cometh, and thy spoil shall be divided in the midst of thee. For I shall gather all nations against Jerusalem to battle; and the city taken, and the houses rifled, and the women ravished.*

## The Plot

By 1817, Denmark had found an ally in Jack Pritchard, or as he was known more familiarly, Gullah Jack. He was owned by Paul Pritchard and lived at 6 Hasell Street. Gullah Jack was a native of Angola and a familiar comical sight on the Charleston streets. He was a short man with bushy side-whiskers who acted like a fool for the whites. Gullah Jack had perfected the "shuck-and-jive" persona. He was a member of the AME church, but also practiced another religion—root, or voodoo. Considered harmless and a fool among the whites, Gullah Jack was known to the blacks as "the little man who can't be killed." A root doctor, who was skilled in the uses of herbs for medicine or poison, could project his mind into others' bodies and could create powerful amulets to protect one against the evils of the world. Gullah Jack was instrumental in spreading the message of Denmark's plan for violent revolution out of the city and into the Sea Island plantations where he traveled frequently. Thus, Denmark could bring two different groups into the fold, the Christian city-dwelling blacks who worked as artisans and household servants and the Gullah island people, all organized with the same plan in mind—freedom or death.

White suspicion of black worship services escalated. Even though they did not discover Denmark's plan for revolution of recruiting soldiers from churches, they were worried about the gathering of such large groups of blacks. Traditional Anglican worship was quiet, subdued and reverential but black worship practices frightened whites. As reported in the *Charleston Times* in 1816:

> *Almost every night there is a meeting of these noisy, frantic worshippers...Midnight! That the meeting of numerous black people to hear the scriptures expounded by an ignorant and (too frequently)*

*vicious person of their own color can be of no benefit either to themselves or the community is certain.*

On December 3, 1817, the city guard (police) raided the AME Church and arrested 469 blacks, charging them with disorderly conduct. But the congregation persevered and on June 9, 1818, the city once again raided the church. This time, 104 free blacks and slaves, including 12 ministers and 1 bishop, were arrested and brought to the guard house. Five of the ministers and the bishop were sentenced to banishment from the state. The other 8 ministers were sentenced to receive ten lashes or pay a fine of five dollars each.

The importance of these raids was to galvanize the commitment among many blacks. Worship was about the only avenue of self-expression among the oppressed and Charleston police ripped that right away from them. When the word of these raids reached the slaves living on the Sea Islands, Gullah Jack remarked that "the Gullah people were ready" to enlist with Vesey's vision of violent rebellion. For the next four years Vesey traveled the Lowcountry area, taking carpenter jobs in remote places and recruiting members of his army and counseling patience. He convinced many of the slaves that the Haitian government would certainly send a black army to aid the Carolina slaves in their revolt. If not that, then after killing their white masters and looting Charleston, the slaves could flee to Haiti. There is little evidence to indicate that Vesey had communication with the Haitian government through second parties, but he managed to convince his recruits that help would come only when the blacks rose against the whites.

Denmark was a mesmerizing figure, manipulating the nationalism, the fears, hopes and religion of the slaves. He preached from the Old Testament and constantly reminded them of the successful Haitian slave rebellion. He also convinced many slaves that there was too large a population of blacks in the area and the white masters had decided the most efficient way to eliminate the surplus was to kill the non-productive, weak, old and infirm. God approved of their plan, Denmark argued. For those who were not Christians, Vesey preached of the sorcerer's skills of Gullah Jack—a man they believed could not be killed and whose charms would keep them from harm.

As 1822 approached, Denmark was almost sixty years old and his attitude had changed. Where he had always tried to live quietly and not attract attention, living as a respectable freed black, he now started to refuse to bow to whites that he passed on the sidewalks. Denmark also had developed a strong disgust for those without the moral strength to stand up for themselves. He began to castigate blacks that did bow, telling them that he "would never cringe to the whites" and that "all men were born equal." When these blacks told him in defense of their actions, "We are slaves," Denmark responded, "You deserve to remain slaves."

By early 1822 Denmark had several chief lieutenants, each of whom had hundreds, if not thousands, of followers who were willing to be led in a violent rebellion. All of Denmark's leaders were slaves, and there were no mulattoes in their ranks. Ned Bennett was a trusted and loved slave in the household of Governor Thomas Bennett who lived at 19 Lynch Street (now Ashley Avenue), less than three blocks from Denmark's home. On the night of the revolt, Ned's job was to seize the state arsenal and distribute the weapons, which included more than two hundred muskets, bayonets and swords. Rolla Bennett was also a slave in service of Governor Bennett. Although Rolla admitted that the governor treated him like a son, he volunteered to murder his master and his family on the night of the rebellion. Yet another trusted slave in the house of the governor was Batteau Bennett. Batteau claimed he would rather murder his master or die violently resisting than continue his life as a privileged slave.

Another slave enlisted in the revolution was Monday Gell. Monday's master, John Gell, owned a livery stable at 127 Church Street and regarded his slave as intelligent and dependable. Monday was an excellent harness maker and his master hired him out to a shop on Meeting Street, letting his slave keep a portion of the earnings for himself. Bacchus Hammett was another early and eager convert to Denmark's vision. He stole a keg of gunpowder, which was hidden for weeks at Denmark's house. Peter Poyas was a ship's carpenter who "wrote in a good hand" and was owned by James Poyas. Poyas lived at 49 King Street and operated a shipyard on Bay Street. Peter had his own weapons and agreed with Denmark, "we are obliged to revolt." Poyas may have been more eager than Denmark for the rebellion to take place. He often urged Denmark that "we cannot go on like this."

By April 1822 word had been spread to the country slaves that the date for the rebellion had been chosen: Sunday, July 14, the anniversary of the storming of the Bastille. Choosing Sunday for the day of rebellion was a brilliant strategic stroke since that was the only day blacks were allowed to congregate in the Market and attend church services. Also, by mid-July, many white militia officers had left town for their summer vacation to Newport, Rhode Island. Thus, there would be fewer experienced military men in town. Dozens of Denmark's trusted aides were collecting weapons, hiding them in strategic locations throughout the city. Blades were being manufactured by slave blacksmiths and hidden in locations around the city. Musket balls were also being made and hidden in bags throughout the city. Gullah Jack reported that the Sea Island slaves were preparing their boats and weapons for the journey to Charleston. Denmark's army was estimated to number almost ten thousand. All around the daily lives of white Charlestonians, preparations were being made for their massacre.

In May 1822, a group of a dozen men gathered for a meeting at Denmark's house on Bull Street to plan the destruction of white Charleston. All who met agreed "nothing could be done without fire." Monday Gell agreed to hide in his harness shop the keg of gunpowder that Bacchus Hammett had stolen. They agreed to set the city on fire at several places, and Denmark told his conspirators that he wanted "every servant in the yards to be ready with axes, knives and clubs, to kill every [white] man as he came out when the [fire] bells rang." Vesey ordered that they were to spare no one—women or children, nor ministers. "Leave no white skin alive," he commanded. And then, quoting Luke 11:23 he said, "'He that is not with me, is against me.'"

While the panic and chaos of the fires would keep most of the whites distracted, the stores of weapons in the city were to be attacked by groups of armed slaves arriving from the south, north and east. Peter Poyas was to lead a group of four thousand coastal blacks from the south up Meeting Street "to seize the City Arsenal and the Guard House opposite St. Michael's Church." At the same time, Gullah Jack was to lead a group from the north and loot the private weapon shops where more than one thousand muskets and bayonets were stored. That group would then join forces with Rolla Bennett's group. The weapons would be distributed and the joined force was to work its way into the city, killing all whites in their way. Groups of slaves from east of the Cooper River were to arrive by boat near the Market and proceed to the guard house killing "every person they might meet, and prevent them from assembling, or extending an alarm." Ned Bennett was given the task of murdering his master and as many members of the family as he could; he was then to walk one block and murder the mayor and his family in their home.

Gullah Jack had instructed his faithful to only eat parched corn and groundnuts on the day of the attack. Jack gave them crab claws they were to hold in their mouths as they attacked, to keep them from being wounded. They believed that once a root doctor, like Gullah Jack, had spoken his incantations over the claws, some of the root doctor's residual power to ward off injury, death or bad luck would be given to them.

On Saturday, May 25, their luck started to change when Peter Priloeau, a house slave of Colonel John Prioleau, was running an errand for his master near the city wharves. He was approached by another black man, a stranger. This other slave asked Peter if he had heard that "something serious was about to take place." Peter replied no and the stranger, later identified as William Paul, replied, "Why, we are determined to shake off our bondage...Many have joined and if you go with me, I will show you the man, who has the list of names, who will take yours down." Peter broke off the conversation and returned home, but a few days later he told his master of the conversation. Colonel Prioleau asked for description of the slave. Prioleau recognized the description of William Paul and on May 31, Paul was arrested at Denmark Vesey's house on Bull Street and placed in the "black hole," which was the solitary confinement of the work house.

Initially Paul claimed ignorance of any plot but by the next day he began to confess. The method of coercion can be easily imagined. Torture by whipping and being kept in the "Crane of Pain." The Crane was a simple, yet effective device. It consisted of two ropes threaded through a pulley and dangling from the ceiling. On the floor beneath the ropes were two shackles. The prisoner's ankles were shackled to the floor and the ropes bound their wrists. The ropes were pulled toward the ceiling, lifting the prisoner's arms, stretching the skin around the ribs. The arms would be pulled higher, higher, until the prisoner was standing on his tiptoes. And just when it seemed it could not go any higher, the ropes were pulled again, yanking the prisoner's arms out of sockets. The prisoner would be left there for hours. And often, he would be whipped with a piece of rawhide, which would flay the skin open.

Paul was kept in the "black hole" and questioned for over a week. He named Peter Poyas, Mingo Harth and Ned Bennett as the chief conspirators. He also knew there was another man involved who was a sorcerer and "carried about him a charm which rendered him invulnerable." Poyas and Harth were arrested and questioned at the work house but both were released. Incredibly, even though Paul was arrested at his house, Denmark was not arrested nor did the authorities suspect him until later.

Governor Bennett did not believe any of the suspected conspiracy. In his opinion, the black population's attitude toward their masters was loving and loyal. Bennett told the mayor that the entire rebellion idea was "nonsense." Indeed, on June 12, his slave Ned Bennett voluntarily turned himself in at the work house. Ned told the wardens that he had heard his name had been mentioned in the investigation of a planned rebellion and he wished to clear his reputation. Ned was questioned for several hours and released. When Ned Bennett was released from the work house, he walked five blocks to Denmark's house to attend a meeting to advance the date of the rebellion before any more investigation could uncover their plot.

The authorities concluded that the allegations of rebellion by Paul had "no confirmation." However, Major John Wilson was not convinced. The major had political ambitions to succeed Bennett as governor. He thought the governor was foolish to be so trustful of the city's slave population. Major Wilson instructed his slave, George Wilson, to inquire among the blacks in Charleston if there was any talk of insurrection. George was a blacksmith who could read and write. George reported to his master on June 14 "that the fact was really so, that a public disturbance was contemplated by the blacks and that not a moment should be lost in informing the authorities, as the succeeding Sunday, the 16$^{th}$, at twelve o'clock at night, was the period fixed for the rising."

Major Wilson informed Mayor James Hamilton of his findings. Hamilton informed Bennett, who gave permission for the captains of the state militia to be summoned. Merely two blocks from Denmark's house, the mayor and the governor were mustering their resources to protect the city. By Sunday night four hundred of the state militia, including horsemen armed with sabers and pistols, were patrolling the streets. The city guard, usually only armed with truncheons, were issued firearms. During the night, most of the white population stayed awake. William Hasell Wilson, son of Major John Wilson, was ten years old in 1822. He later wrote in 1902: "I shall never forget the feeling of alarm and anxiety that pervaded the whole community...no one, not even the children ventured to retire."

On Monday, June 17, the city council convened to consider how to best safeguard the city. They appointed a committee for "exploring the causes and character of the existing disturbance, and bringing to light and punishment the suspected and guilty."

Peter Poyas, Ned Bennett and Rolla and Batteau Bennett were arrested the next day, as well as six others, but not Denmark. Vesey knew that his conspirators would sooner or later reveal his name to the authorities, so he burned all written records of the conspiracy, left his Bull Street house and went into hiding in the house of one of his wives. He was hoping to stow away on a ship leaving Charleston. By Saturday, June 22, the authorities were actively seeking Denmark Vesey. Peter Poyas was chained to a pole in the work house with another of the conspirators. For several hours the blacks were promised, cajoled and then threatened and tortured, but neither man revealed anything.

Someone broke down however, for several days later Captain Dove of the city guard broke into the house of Vesey's wife and he was arrested. He was taken to the work house to await trial.

## The Trial

Justice for blacks was different than justice for whites in Charleston in 1822. There was no trial by jury. Instead, blacks were tried before a group of judges; the verdict did not have to be unanimous. There was no requirement that counsel be present. The Duke de la Rochefoucauld-Liancourt commented on South Carolina slave justice:

> *No defender is allowed to the poor wretched accused; and his judges have the power to condemn him to whatever mode of death they think proper. Simple theft by a Negro is punished with death...For the murder of a Negro...a white man pays a fine of three thousand six hundred and eighty dollars. If he had only beaten the Negro...the fine is but one thousand five hundred dollars. He who maims a Negro, puts out his eyes, cuts off his tongue, or castrates him, pays only a fine of four hundred and twenty-eight dollars. A Negro slaying a white man...wound a white man...he will eventually be put to death.*

On June 19, court opened and the trials began. Over the next seven days, a total of 131 blacks were arrested; 15 were acquitted and 38 others were discharged after serving a prison sentence and enduring whippings at the work house. Forty-three others were "transported" (moved to other states as slaves at their owner's expense) and 5 slaves who testified against the other conspirators were allowed to live. The other 34 were hanged within a month.

The first group of six was sentenced to be hanged on July 2, between the hours of six and eight in the morning. On the appointed morning the *City Gazette* published a notice of the execution. A huge crowd of blacks and whites gathered near the gallows, located on Blake's Land (present location of I-26 and Meeting Street). The prisoners were marched to their death chained at their legs and wrists.

Those who were executed on July 2, 1822, were: Batteau Bennett, Ned Bennett, Rolla Bennett, Jesse Blackwood, Peter Poyas and Denmark Vesey. Ten days later, on July 12, Gullah Jack Pritchard and John Horry were executed. Gullah Jack was accused of not only planning to massacre white Charleston, but also to have "endeavored to enlist on your behalf all the powers of darkness." During the trial John Horry testified that he had a sword. When asked by his owner, Elias Horry, what he intended to do with it John replied, "to rip open your belly." On July 26, 1822, twenty-two more men were executed, including:

*Smart Anderson:*
*Smart was a drayman who stole two muskets, hiding them on his cart to be used when the occasion arose. He claimed he was in the rebellion "as much as possible."*

*Charles Billings:*
*Worked in a commercial stable and planned to steal horses on the night of the rebellion. He claimed that he was "ready and willing" to do what needed to be done.*

*Jemmy Clement:*
*Member of the AME Church*

*Jerry Cohen:*
*One of the last arrested, he claimed that if everyone involved was killed, he was "still willing to go on."*

*Polydore Faber:*

*A good friend of Gullah Jack, Polydore was convicted of hiding at least twenty pike poles that were to be fitted with blades and used as weapons on the night of rebellion.*

*Julius Forrest:*

*Claimed to have been "charmed" by Gullah Jack into joining the rebellion.*

*Lot Forrester:*

*One of the most active of Denmark's recruits. He worked at the state arsenal and was able to steal a slow fuse to be used in setting fires throughout the city.*

*Jack Glenn:*

*Although he was lame in both feet, he told Vesey he would serve as a horseman on the night of rebellion. He collected money about town to finance the plot.*

*Bacchus Hammett:*

*Stole a keg of black powder, a sword and pistol for the rebellion. On his way to the gallows he shocked the white crowd by laughing and shouting good-byes to his acquaintances. Upon his execution, the mechanism failed, and he did not drop. According to a witness, Bacchus "threw himself forward, and as he swung back he lifted his feet, so that his knees might not touch the Board." He was shot with a pistol by Captain Dove because he was taking so long to die dangling from the gallows.*

*Mingo Harth:*

*He was a skilled laborer and worked at a lumberyard. Mingo hosted Bible study classes in his quarters in order to discuss the rebellion.*

*Joe Jore:*

*Joe, even though he was considered an invalid, pledged to take a sword and fight on the night of rebellion.*

*Dean Mitchell:*

*Assisted in collecting money to make spears and pikes.*

*Jack Purcell:*

*Though he was one of Denmark's first recruits, on the gallows he stated that "if it had not been for the cunning of that old villain, Vesey, I should not now be in my present situation."*

*Adam Robertson:*

*To prove his commitment to the rebellion, he participated in a ceremony where everyone present ate a bloody chicken.*

*John Robertson:*

*Also participated in the chicken ceremony.*

*Robert Robertson:*

*He helped conceal pikes and spears, and also stole a pistol from his master.*

*Tom Russell:*

*A blacksmith who forged pike heads and spears as long as the group took up a collection to pay for the materials. Tom was also trained by Gullah Jack to be a sorcerer.*

*Dick Simms:*

*Dick stole a pistol from his master, novelist William Gilmore Simms, to use during the rebellion.*

*Pharo Thompson:*

*Pharo possessed a sword fashioned out of a scythe.*

*Adam Yates:*

*Adam had the responsibility of leading the rural blacks into the city on the night of rebellion.*

*Bellisle Yates:*

*Bellisle was responsible for hiding some of the plantation blacks in the city during the night of rebellion.*

*Naphur Yates:*

*Naphur took an oath and swore that his "heart was in this business." He claimed that his name had ordained him to be part of the rebellion since the word Naphur is defined in the Bible as "purification fire."*

More executions took place on July 12, 1822, than on any other day in Charleston history. The entire city turned out for the Friday morning spectacle. There was such a large crowd and so much excitement that a small black boy was trampled to death.

Executions continued on July 30, 1822, with the deaths of Jack McNeil, Tom Scott Caesar Smith and Jacob Stagg. The last to be executed was William Garner on August 9, 1822. He was to lead a group of horsemen into the city on the night of rebellion. Garner escaped to Columbia when the first group was arrested, but later was arrested after the governor had offered a $200 reward for his capture.

The bodies of all the convicted were given to the Medical College of South Carolina for dissection.

# Chapter Six

# The Code of Dis-Honor

*Duels are a murderous practice. They decide nothing.*
Benjamin Franklin

## General Daniel Edgar Sickles—Eminent Scoundrel

General Daniel Sickles (1819–1914) was appointed to the military governorship of South Carolina in late 1865. He left his sickly wife Teresa in New York and arrived by steamer with prodigious powers. The only restraint upon him was the president's cabinet and the hostile acceptance in South Carolina. Sickles was, in effect, a virtual dictator within the state. He found Charleston a demoralized city. Part of the town was in rubble due to the 1861 fire and the 587-day Union bombardment. But despite that the city had not lost its fighting hubris. The only wealthy people were profiteers and Yankee investors. Sickles was once described as possessing "the wisdom of Solomon, the patience of Job, and the audacity of the Devil" and in dealing with the Reconstruction of South Carolina, he would need all three. He knew it was a hotbed of violence and intrigue as his comments indicate:

> *Charleston has much intelligence and considerable genuine culture; but go twenty miles away and you are in the land of barbarians . . . In South Carolina there is very little pretense of loyalty. I believe I found less than fifty men who admitted any love for the Union. I have not seen an American flag raised by a Carolinian. If one floated over a dwelling, or a hotel or a shop, the population would avoid the place as they would shun a pesthouse filled with lepers.*

Sickles arrived in Charleston an infamous man. Long before his heroics in the war, Sickles had been a national figure for a spectacular murder trial and an international scandal.

Sickles was a notorious womanizer. Even after he married the much-younger Teresa Bagioli, daughter of an Italian music teacher, he continued his wenching. Through his contacts, Sickles was appointed assistant to Ambassador James Buchanan in England. He left his young pregnant wife behind (she would later join him after the birth of a daughter) and in her stead he took as his companion his favorite New York madam. While in London, representing the American embassy, he attended a function at Buckingham Palace with his New York madam, giving Sickles the unique distinction of being the first (and only) American diplomat to present a whore to the Queen.

As a young man Sickles worked in the law office of Benjamin Butler, who at the time was attorney general in President Van Buren's cabinet. Later Sickles served several terms in Congress and in the New York State Senate. While Sickles was serving in Congress, he lived across from the White House on Lafayette Park, and in 1859 he became involved in one of the most notorious murder trials in American history. During President James Buchanan's inauguration, Teresa Sickles met the United States attorney for the District of Columbia, Philip Barton Key, whose father was Francis Scott Key, the author of "The Star-Spangled Banner." Although Key was a widower with four young children he apparently was something of a lothario. He became involved with Teresa Sickles using a rented house in the city for their private meetings. But in February Sickles discovered that his wife was having secret "assignations," and on February 27, Sickles confronted Key at the corner of Pennsylvania Avenue and Madison Place. After a few seconds of shouting, Sickles pulled out a pistol. The first two shots missed, but the third struck Keys.

He fell to the ground, mortally wounded. Sickles walked to the man and shot him once more, in view of two witnesses.

The killing preoccupied the public. It became the equivalent of today's high-profile celebrity trials. Each morning people waited for the newspapers so they could devour the latest twist and turn of the trial. The *New York Daily News* noted that the "tragedy is the absorbing topic of conversation, the never-tiring subject of eager and fierce discussion." An article in the March 12, 1859 edition of *Harper's Weekly* concluded that Sickles was justified in killing the man who seduced his wife, and predicted that no jury in the United States would convict him, even of manslaughter.

Sickles was indicted on March 24 and his trial began on April 4, with five jurors selected. On April 5 the court went through a panel of seventy-five potential jurors, finding only two additional who were qualified to serve. Seventy were discharged because they had formed opinions of the case and could not give a fair verdict. Edwin Stanton, who later became Abraham Lincoln's secretary of war, represented Sickles. Stanton had invented a novel defense called "temporary insanity"—extremely temporary insanity, as it proved, because had it lasted longer than a day or two, Mr. Sickles might have been obliged to resign from Congress.

The courtroom was packed with spectators, many of whom had to stand on tiptoe to catch a glimpse of the proceedings. The trial lasted for twenty-one days. Despite the lengthy trial, the jury deliberated for barely over an hour before coming back with a verdict of not guilty. Sickles's admirers carried him out of the courtroom. The trial marked the first time in which temporary insanity was used as a defense. After his acquittal, Sickles took his wife back. He told his critics:

> *I am not aware of any statute or code of morals which makes it infamous to forgive a woman. I can now see in the almost universal denunciation with which she is followed to my threshold the misery and peril from which I have rescued the mother of my daughter. I shall strive to prove to all that an erring wife and mother may be forgiven and redeemed.*

General Sickles arrived as military governor of South Carolina after the War between the States and set up living quarters in a Charlotte Street mansion in Charleston. He made his military headquarters at the Citadel (present-day 337 Meeting Street). There was an elected South Carolina governor, James Orr, but there was no question who was in charge. Sickles had a force of 352 officers and 7,000 men, and he gave a mandate that this force should be deployed to protect the freed blacks and loyal whites from the anger of Confederate veterans. President Andrew Johnson did not like Sickles. He considered the general a radical who was too independent, and Johnson looked for ways to remove Sickles from his post.

On January 1, 1866, Sickles issued a general order that the state's Black Code was null and void: "All laws shall be applicable to all inhabitants." That order did little to endear Sickles to most of the white population of the state. But it seemed to have little effect on the attitude and behavior of many white women.

Sickles issued another order that restricted the manufacture of liquor in order to keep more grain available as food. President Johnson did not approve of Sickles's heavy-handed dealing of the South Carolina problems without his approval. Johnson grew to hate Sickles, calling him "a conceited cuckold." Johnson removed Sickles on August 12, 1867. The *Charleston Mercury* stated: "We affirm that here in this city there was a universal felling of relief at his departure."

During the spring of 1869 President Ulysses S. Grant appointed Sickles the United States minister to Spain, a post that he retained until March 20, 1874. Once in Madrid, Sickles began an affair with Queen Isabella and became known as the "The Yankee King of Spain." He later married Senorita Carmina Creagh, the daughter of a Spanish counselor of state, Chevalier de Creagh of Madrid.

He never returned to Charleston and at age ninety-one, Sickles died at his home on 23 Fifth Avenue in New York City. He is buried at Arlington National Cemetery, having made his mark not only on Charleston and South Carolina, but also on the entire politics of America.

# Fools in a Duel: Settling Affairs of Honor

From a modern perspective, a duel may seem to be the most absurd manner in which to settle an argument, but at one point it was an accepted, and even celebrated, practice for gentlemen to settle "affairs of honor." South Carolina, along with Georgia, Mississippi and Tennessee, were the renowned states for dueling. The South Carolina social and plantation system cultivated pride and personal honor. The typical South Carolina gentleman was "quick to resent an insult and slow to forgive an injury." Often, duels were fought over trifle instances.

In 1832, Mr. Roach and Mr. Adams were two students at the South Carolina College. During a meal at the mess hall they grabbed hold of the same dish of food at the same time. Both refused to release their claim, and the argument grew to a point where a challenge was issued. The two men squared off. Roach was wounded, but managed to kill Adams. Full of remorse Roach drank himself to death during the next few years.

Dueling at one time was so accepted in Charleston that even men of the cloth were not immune to participation in duels. In 1795, the Reverend Henry Purcell, rector of St. Michael's Church, challenged a fellow clergyman for condemning a pamphlet Purcell had written against Bishop Samuel Seabury. An organization called the Ten Paces Club was formed and one assumes it had a dwindling membership. Most men could not decline to fight, unless they had already killed another man in a previous duel; however, not everyone approved of dueling. General Charles Cotesworth Pinckney, a Charleston lawyer, Revolutionary hero and signer of the Constitution, spoke out against the practice: "Is there no way of abolishing this absurd and barbaric practice? Dueling is no criteria of bravery." Many of Pinckney's contemporaries agreed. General Zachary Taylor said of dueling, "I have served in the army forty years without fighting a duel. I shall have no dueling man about me, if I can help it." Henry Clay's feelings were similar: "No man would be happier than myself to see the whole barbarous system for ever eradicated." Benjamin Franklin also saw duels as having no honor or validity: "Duels are a murderous practice. They decide nothing."

Ironically, Alexander Hamilton was quoted saying, "My religious and moral principles are strongly opposed to dueling—I abhor the practice." Of course, that opinion did not keep Hamilton from being killed by Aaron Burr in the swamps of New Jersey in the most famous duel in American history. Burr, the sitting vice president, was a hunted man for several months. Burr had many links to Charleston and South Carolina. His daughter, Theodosia, had married into the prominent Alston family of Charleston. Vice President Burr's best friend from the U.S. Senate was Pierce Butler, another South Carolinian signer of the Constitution. Burr hid out for months on Butler's vast plantation properties in South Carolina and Georgia.

Like many early American customs, dueling was imported. It started in the Middle Ages when European nobles defended their honor in man-to-man battles. An early version of dueling was known as "judicial combat," so called because God allegedly judged the man in the right and let him win. In an era known for its bloody encounters, judicial combats probably prevented men from killing in the heat of passion. Still, heads of state, the Catholic Church and other numerous authorities tried, with little effect, to ban dueling.

In 1777, a group of Irishmen codified dueling practices in a document entitled *Code Duello*. The code contained twenty-five specific rules outlining all aspects of the duel. An Americanized version of the code, written by South Carolina Governor John Lyde Wilson, appeared in 1838. Prior to that, Americans made do with the European rules. Wilson's stated intention was to prevent "unnecessary" deaths. To accomplish that all the planning was to be done by persons known as "seconds," who presumably would have the distance and clarity to keep emotions from getting involved. At least one night must intervene between an offense and the duel. The seconds were always encouraged to propose shaking hands. A man refusing to fight was posted as a coward. Duels were almost the exclusive domain of the aristocracy and due to the delicate, personal nature of the event, most were never mentioned in the press.

Most duelists chose guns as their weapons. The large-caliber, smoothbore flintlock pistols Burr and Hamilton used in their encounter typified the American dueling weapons. The chance of dying in a pistol duel was relatively slim as flintlocks often misfired. Even in the hands of an experienced shooter, accuracy was difficult. Generally, pistols had to be discharged within three seconds; to take aim for a longer time period was considered dishonorable.

By the time of the Burr-Hamilton duel, the practice had begun to decline in the North. In the South though, dueling remained the gentleman's way to defend his honor, or to get away with murder. A gentleman with vindication on his mind had only to wait for a rival's insult. He was then free to challenge and kill the rival without condemnation.

Many others feared a duel. A word or two passed in private company on a Friday night could well mean a challenge on Saturday morning and death on Sunday. Avoiding a challenge wasn't easy, particularly in Charleston, where men who refused to duel would be "posted." A statement accusing them of cowardice would be hung in public areas or published in a newspaper or pamphlet.

Dueling was still in vogue in Charleston in 1828 when Bishop John England gave an address to the Anti-Dueling Society of Charleston, in the Cathedral of St. Finbar. Bishop England was of the opinion that "the good sense and sober judgment of the vast majority of upright and educated men are altogether opposed to the practice of dueling, as not only useless for society, but as criminal and mischievous in its results." He noted that the derivation of the word duel comes from the Latin words *Duellum,* meaning as it were, and *bellum inter duo* or *duorum bellum,* meaning war between two persons.

But by the time of the Civil War, dueling had begun to decline, even in the South. Public opinion turned against the practice. After the violence and the staggering loss of male life during the war, most people began to see dueling for what it truly was—a foolish, wasteful and bloody practice.

## Notable South Carolina Duels

*Henry Laurens v. J.F. Grimke*:

This was the height of foolishness; the old man Laurens against the youthful, soon-to-be Judge Grimke. Grimke had the right to fire first but his pistol misfired. Laurens, who opposed dueling, refused to take his turn. In disgust Laurens tossed his pistol at the feet of the younger man and with the help of his second and a walking cane, he shuffled off toward his waiting carriage. Grimke spent several minutes urging Laurens to "take a shot, old man, or draw your sword!" Laurens drove off in his carriage, ignoring the young Grimke's shouts The duel was concluded by Laurens's second after declaring that Grimke's challenge had been met.

*Edward Simons v. Thomas Geddes*:

During a Charleston political campaign in 1823, Simons "damned" General John Geddes and his son, Thomas. During the duel, the first four shots cut the two men's clothing. At the fifth round Geddes was shot in the thigh and Simons was killed.

*Taber v. Magrath*:

Articles printed in the *Charleston Mercury* in 1856 signed by "Nullifier" (Edmund Rhett) attacked Judge A.G. Magrath of being of "bankrupt character." An editorial note accompanying the articles indicated that the paper endorsed the sentiment. Magrath was running for Congress, and his younger brother, Edward, challenged the editors, Taber and Heart, to a duel. Both men accepted.

Taber claimed he must defend the liberty of the press. Taber's second, Cunningham, claimed they had come to "seek satisfaction as well as give it." The first and second shots gave no satisfaction, and after an hour-long argument, the principals were in place for a third shot. Taber was mortally wounded in the third round. The second duel between Magrath and Heart did not occur.

*Ladd v. Issacs*:

Dr. Joseph Ladd arrived in Charleston from Rhode Island in 1785 to begin his medical practice. Even though medicine was his profession, he was a poet at heart. He arrived in Charleston looking at the change in his life through the eyes and temperament of an artist, not as a scientist. The stagecoach dropped him off on Bay Street that evening and he walked several blocks to an inn to inquire about lodgings.

Dr. Ladd had a habit of whistling as he walked. He whistled as he strolled down the dark street when suddenly two robbers accosted him. One pulled a knife and demanded money. Luckily Ralph Issacs was walking the street that night also and he intervened, pulling his own pistol. He managed to scare away the would-be thieves and escorted the doctor to the inn where Ladd insisted on buying Issacs a meal and drinks. By the end of the evening the two men were fast friends.

Dr. Ladd found permanent lodging in the home of two old sisters, Fannie and Della Rose. Ladd was an attractive, intelligent and charming man and soon became a delight for the old women. They could hear him in his room every morning, whistling as he dressed. They would listen to him leave in the morning whistling, and they always knew when he was returning home because his whistling arrived a moment before he did. The two old women doted on their lodger, treating him as a beloved son or nephew. They introduced the doctor to their large circle of friends. In short order, Dr. Ladd was in high demand on the Charleston social scene.

Issacs, a lifetime Charleston resident, soon began to resent the doctor's standing in the community. In a few short months, Dr. Ladd had risen to the heights of the social scene, something Issacs had not managed to do during his entire lifetime. As Dr. Ladd's social circle increased the two men, once friends, spent less time together. To make matters worse, Dr. Ladd began to escort a Charleston lady to social gatherings, a lady that Isaacs himself had spent several months courting.

Finally, the jealousy was too much for Issacs and he wrote a letter to the editor of the *Charleston Gazette* in which he called Ladd "as blasted a scoundrel as ever disgraced humanity." Fearing his reputation might be damaged, and urged by friends that a gentleman would be posted as a coward if he did not respond to the offense, Ladd challenged Issacs to a duel, against his better judgment.

The morning of the duel the two men met in Philadelphia Alley. Yet when confronted with each other, Ladd could not follow through. He fired his first shot into the air. Issacs, however, shot Ladd in the leg to cripple him. At least, that was his intention. His shot went high and Dr. Ladd was hit in the stomach. His friends carried him back to the house where the Rose sisters nursed him for over a week, but Dr. Joseph Ladd never recovered. He died ten days after the duel.

# *Code Duello*: The Rules of Dueling by Governor John Lyde Wilson

**Rule 1.**

*The first offense requires the first apology, though the retort may have been more offensive than the insult. Example: A tells B he is impertinent, etc. B retorts that he lies; yet A must make the first apology because he gave the first offense, and then (after one fire) B may explain away the retort by a subsequent apology.*

**Rule 2.**

*But if the parties would rather fight on, then after two shots each (but in no case before), B may explain first, and A apologize afterward.*

*N.B. The above rules apply to all cases of offenses in retort not of stronger class than the example.*

**Rule 3.**

*If a doubt exist who gave the first offense, the decision rests with the seconds; if they won't decide, or can't agree, the matter must proceed to two shots, or to a hit, if the challenger require it.*

**Rule 4.**

*When the lie direct is the first offense, the aggressor must either beg pardon in express terms; exchange two shots previous to apology; or three shots followed up by explanation; or fire on till a severe hit be received by one party or the other.*

**Rule 5.**

*As a blow is strictly prohibited under any circumstances among gentlemen, no verbal apology can be received for such an insult. The alternatives, therefore—the offender handing a cane to the injured party, to be used on his own back, at the same time begging pardon; firing on until one or both are disabled; or exchanging three shots, and then asking pardon without proffer of the cane.*

*If swords are used, the parties engage until one is well blooded, disabled, or disarmed; or until, after receiving a wound, and blood being drawn, the aggressor begs pardon.*

*N.B. A disarm is considered the same as a disable. The disarmer may (strictly) break his adversary's sword; but if it be the challenger who is disarmed, it is considered as ungenerous to do so.*

*In the case the challenged be disarmed and refuses to ask pardon or atone, he must not be killed, as formerly; but the challenger may lay his own sword on the aggressor's shoulder, then break the aggressor's sword and say, "I spare your life!" The challenged can never revive the quarrel—the challenger may.*

**Rule 6.**

*If A gives B the lie, and B retorts by a blow (being the two greatest offenses), no reconciliation can take place till after two discharges each, or a severe hit; after which B may beg A's pardon humbly for the blow and then A may explain simply for the lie; because a blow is never allowable, and the offense of the lie, therefore, merges in it. (See preceding rules.)*

*N.B. Challenges for undivulged causes may be reconciled on the ground, after one shot. An explanation or the slightest hit should be sufficient in such cases, because no personal offense transpired.*

**Rule 7.**

*But no apology can be received, in any case, after the parties have actually taken ground, without exchange of fires.*

**Rule 8.**

*In the above case, no challenger is obliged to divulge his cause of challenge (if private) unless required by the challenged so to do before their meeting.*

**Rule 9.**

*All imputations of cheating at play, races, etc., to be considered equivalent to a blow; but may be reconciled after one shot, on admitting their falsehood and begging pardon publicly.*

**Rule 10.**

*Any insult to a lady under a gentleman's care or protection to be considered as, by one degree, a greater offense than if given to the gentleman personally, and to be regulated accordingly.*

**Rule 11.**

*Offenses originating or accruing from the support of ladies' reputations, to be considered as less unjustifiable than any others of the same class, and as admitting of slighter apologies by the aggressor: this to be determined by the circumstances of the case, but always favorable to the lady.*

**Rule 12.**
*In simple, unpremeditated recontres with the smallsword, or couteau de chasse, the rule is—first draw, first sheath, unless blood is drawn; then both sheath, and proceed to investigation.*

**Rule 13.**
*No dumb shooting or firing in the air is admissible in any case. The challenger ought not to have challenged without receiving offense; and the challenged ought, if he gave offense, to have made an apology before he came on the ground; therefore, children's play must be dishonorable on one side or the other, and is accordingly prohibited.*

**Rule 14.**
*Seconds to be of equal rank in society with the principals they attend, inasmuch as a second may either choose or chance to become a principal, and equality is indispensible.*

**Rule 15.**
*Challenges are never to be delivered at night, unless the party to be challenged intend leaving the place of offense before morning; for it is desirable to avoid all hot-headed proceedings.*

**Rule 16.**
*The challenged has the right to choose his own weapon, unless the challenger gives his honor he is no swordsman; after which, however, he can decline any second species of weapon proposed by the challenged.*

**Rule 17.**
*The challenged chooses his ground; the challenger chooses his distance; the seconds fix the time and terms of firing.*

**Rule 18.**
*The seconds load in presence of each other, unless they give their mutual honors they have charged smooth and single, which should be held sufficient.*

**Rule 19.**

*Firing may be regulated—first by signal; secondly, by word of command; or thirdly, at pleasure—as may be agreeable to the parties. In the latter case, the parties may fire at their reasonable leisure, but second presents and rests are strictly prohibited.*

**Rule 20.**

*In all cases a miss-fire is equivalent to a shot, and a snap or non-cock is to be considered as a miss-fire.*

**Rule 21.**

*Seconds are bound to attempt a reconciliation before the meeting takes place, or after sufficient firing or hits, as specified.*

**Rule 22.**

*Any wound sufficient to agitate the nerves and necessarily make the hand shake, must end the business for that day.*

**Rule 23.**

*If the cause of the meeting be of such a nature that no apology or explanation can or will be received, the challenged takes his ground, and calls on the challenger to proceed as he chooses; in such cases, firing at pleasure is the usual practice, but may be varied by agreement.*

**Rule 24.**

*In slight cases, the second hands his principal but one pistol; but in gross cases, two, holding another case ready charged in reserve.*

**Rule 25.**

*Where seconds disagree, and resolve to exchange shots themselves, it must be at the same time and at right angles with their principals.*

*Author's Note: And you thought the fine print on your car lease agreement was confusing!*

# Author's Note

Throughout the manuscript two different spellings in reference to Charleston have been used. In its early years (prior to 1717) the city was called, and written as Charles Town. After the city was incorporated in 1783, it was called Charleston. I have tried to be consistent in the use of the two names of the city, using the proper term for the time period of each story.

# Appendix

## 1718 Pirate Executions

| Name | Race | Sex | Occupation | Crime | Method | Date |
|---|---|---|---|---|---|---|
| ROBINSON, Edward | W | M | Pirate | Piracy | Hanging | Nov. 8 |
| PATTERSON, Neal | W | M | Pirate | Piracy | Hanging | Nov. 8 |
| SCOT, William | W | M | Pirate | Piracy | Hanging | Nov. 8 |
| BAYLEY, Job | W | M | Pirate | Piracy | Hanging | Nov. 8 |
| SMITH, John | W | M | Pirate | Piracy | Hanging | Nov. 8 |
| THOMAS, John | W | M | Pirate | Piracy | Hanging | Nov. 8 |
| HEWET, William | W | M | Pirate | Piracy | Hanging | Nov. 8 |
| EDDY, William | W | M | Pirate | Piracy | Hanging | Nov. 8 |

# Appendix

| Name | Race | Sex | Occupation | Crime | Method | Date |
|---|---|---|---|---|---|---|
| ANNAND, Alexander | W | M | Pirate | Piracy | Hanging | Nov. 8 |
| ROSS, George | W | M | Pirate | Piracy | Hanging | Nov. 8 |
| DUNKIN, George | W | M | Pirate | Piracy | Hanging | Nov. 8 |
| KING, Matthew | W | M | Pirate | Piracy | Hanging | Nov. 8 |
| PERRY, Daniel | W | M | Pirate | Piracy | Hanging | Nov. 8 |
| VIRGIN, Henry | W | M | Pirate | Piracy | Hanging | Nov. 8 |
| ROBBINS, James | W | M | Pirate | Piracy | Hanging | Nov. 8 |
| MULLET, James | W | M | Pirate | Piracy | Hanging | Nov. 8 |
| PRICE, Thomas | W | M | Pirate | Piracy | Hanging | Nov. 8 |
| LOPEZ, John | W | M | Pirate | Piracy | Hanging | Nov. 8 |
| LONG, Zachariah | W | M | Pirate | Piracy | Hanging | Nov. 8 |
| BONNET, Stede | W | M | Pirate | Piracy | Hanging | Dec. 10 |

# Bibliography

American Council of Learned Societies. *American National Biography*. London: Oxford University Press, Inc., 2000.

Baker, Bishop Robert J. "Religion and Public Life: In the Days of Bishop John England: The Dueling Controversy." www.catholic-doc.org.

Baker Susan. "Anne Bonny & Mary Read" in *Women Remembered*, ed. Nancy Myron and Charlotte Bunch. Diana Press, 1974.

Bolton, S. Charles. *Southern Anglicanism: The Church of England in Colonial South Carolina*. Westport, Connecticut: Greenwood Press, 1982.

Bragg, Melvyn. *The Adventures of English: 500 AD to 2000*. Princeton, New Jersey: Films for the Humanities and Sciences, 2004.

Branch, Muriel Miller. *The Water Brought Us: The Story of the Gullah-Speaking People*. Orangeburg, South Carolina: Sandlapper Publishing Company, Inc., 1995.

Charleston *Courier*, 1819–1820.

City Council. *Negro Plot: An Account of the Late Intended Insurrection Among A Portion of the Blacks of the City of Charleston, South Carolina.* Boston: Joseph W. Ingaham, 1822. Published by the Authority of the Corporation of Charleston.

Coote, Stephen. *Royal Survivor: The Life of Charles II.* New York: St. Martin's Press, 2000.

Cordingly, David, ed. *Pirates: Terror on the High Seas—From the Caribbean to the South China Sea*. Atlanta, Georgia: Turner Publishing, Inc., 1996.

———. *Under the Black Flag*. New York: Random House, 1995.

———. *Women Sailors & Sailors' Women.* New York: Random House, 2001.

Edgar, Walter. *South Carolina: A History.* Columbia: University of South Carolina Press, 1998.

Fraser, Walter J. *Charleston! Charleston! The History of a Southern City.* Columbia: University of South Carolina Press, 1989.

Gillespie, Joanna Bowen. *The Life and Times of Martha Laurens Ramsay 1756–1811.* Columbia: University of South Carolina Press, 2001.

Haley, K.H.D. *The First Earl of Shaftsbury*. London: Oxford University Press, 1968.

Hogue, L. Lynn. *An Edition of "Eight Charges Delivered, At So Many Several General Sessions, & Gaol Deliveries: Held At Charles Town...In The Years 1703, 1704, 1705, 1706, 1707...By Nicholas Trott Esq; Chief Justice of the Province of South Carolina."* Ann Arbor, Michigan: UMI Dissertation Services, 1972.

Jacoby, Mary Moore, ed. *The Churches of Charleston and the Lowcountry.* Columbia: University of South Carolina Press, 1994.

Johnson, Captain Charles [Daniel Defoe]. *A General History of the Robberies and Murders of the Most Notorious Pirates*. 1724.

*Journal of the Council*. Series: 213019, vol. 0039, p. 28. South Carolina Department of Archives and History, Columbia, South Carolina.

Keneally, Thomas. *American Scoundrel*. New York: Doubleday, 2002.

Klingberg, Frank J. *The Carolina Chronicle of Dr. Francis Le Jau, 1706–1717*. Berkeley: University of California Press, 1956.

Lander, Ernest Mcpherson. *A History of South Carolina, 1865–1960*. Columbia, South Carolina: The University of South Carolina Press, 1970.

Lofton, John. *Denmark Vesey's Revolt: The Slave Plot That Lit a Fuse to Fort Sumter*. Kent, Ohio: The Kent State University Press, 1983.

Longacre, Edward G. *Gentleman and Solder: The Extraordinary Life of General Wade Hampton*. Nashville, Tennessee: Rutledge Hill Press, 2003.

Marren, Albert. *The Sea Rovers: Pirates, Privateers and Buccaneers*. New York: Athenum, 1984.

McCrady, Edward. *The History of South Carolina Under the Proprietary Government, 1670–1719*. 1897. Reprinted, New York: Russell & Russell, 1969.

———. *The History of South Carolina Under the Royal Government, 1719–1776*. 1897. Reprinted, New York: Russell & Russell, 1969.

Miles, Suzannah Smith. "Madeira M'dear." *Charleston Magazine*: December 2004.

*Minutes of the South Carolina Court of Common Pleas*. South Carolina Department Archives and History, Columbia, South Carolina.

Pearson, Edward A. *Designs Against Charleston: The Trial Record of the Denmark Vesey Conspiracy of 1822.* Chapel Hill: University of North Carolina Press, 1999.

Pease, Jane H. and William H. *Ladies, Women & Wenches.* Chapel Hill: The University of North Carolina Press. 1990.

Pike, James S. *The Prostrate State.* New York: Loring and Mussey, 1935.

Poole, Jason. "On Borrowed Ground: Free African-American life in Charleston, South Carolina 1810–61." *Essays in History* 36 (1994).

Ramsay, David. *The History of South-Carolina from its First Settlement in 1670, to the Year 1808.* Charleston: David Longworth, 1809.

Ravenel, Beatrice St. Julien, ed. *Charleston Murders.* New York: Duell, Sloan and Pierce. 1947.

Rhyne, Nancy. *Slave Ghost Stories.* Orangeburg: Sandlapper Publishing Company, Inc., 2002.

Ripley, Warren. "Charles Towne: Birth of a City. Charleston, South Carolina." Charleston, South Carolina: *Post and Courier,* 1970.

Robertson, David. *Denmark Vesey: The Buried History of America's Largest Slave Rebellion and the Man Who Led It.* New York: Alfred A. Knopf, Inc., 1999.

Rosen, Robert. *A Short History of Charleston.* Columbia: University of South Carolina Press, 1992.

Sabine, Lorenzo. *Notes on Duels and Dueling.* Boston: Crosby, Nichols and Co., 1855.

Swanberg, W.A. *Sickles the Incredible.* Gettysburg, Pennsylvania: Stan Clark Military Books, 1956.

Taylor, Rayford Boles. "The South Carolina Judiciary, 1669–1769." Ph.D. diss., University of Michigan, 1978.

Thompson, Henry T. *Ousting the Carpetbagger From South Carolina.* Columbia: R.L. Bryan Company, 1927.

Wallace, David Duncan. *South Carolina: A Short History, 1520–1948.* Columbia: University of South Carolina Press, 1951.

Williams Jack Kenny. *Vogues in Villany.* Columbia: University of South Carolina Press, 1959.

———. "Crime and Punishment in South Carolina, 1790–1860." Ph.D. diss., University of Michigan, 1953.

Woodmason, Charles. *The Carolina Backcountry.* Chapel Hill: University of North Carolina Press, 1953.

# About the Author

Mark R. Jones is a ninth-generation native of South Carolina, part of an old Charleston family—not a *rich* old Charleston family. Part of his family heritage includes a kinship with Daniel Boone and President Abraham Lincoln. He is a licensed, active City of Charleston tour guide, conducting carriage tours for Palmetto Carriage. He is also the owner of Black Cat Tours, which specializes in adult-oriented nighttime walking tours, featuring the Wicked Walk. On average, Mark conducts more than twenty tours per week. In his spare time he likes to read, research more wicked events and spend time with novelist Rebel Sinclair and their two cats—Edgar Allan Poe and Annabel Lee.

For more information on Mark and his tours, visit:

www.acharlestontourguide.com
www.blackcattours.com
www.wickedcharleston.net

www.ingramcontent.com/pod-product-compliance
Lightning Source LLC
LaVergne TN
LVHW020511100826
845148LV00003B/755